A MILLION YEARS

Finding God's Highest Purpose
in Your Spiritual Wilderness

Beverly A. Price

"By and by, when the morning comes,
when the saints of God are gathered home,
We will tell the story,
how we've overcome,
we will understand it better by and by."

Lyrics by: Charles Albert Tindley

"When The Morning Comes"
(1905)

A Million Years: Finding God's Highest Purpose
In Your Spiritual Wilderness

The Beverly Price Company

Published in the United States of America

ISBN: 979-8-218-17907-6

DEDICATION

Unto Him Who Is Able

PREFACE

It appeared the sun wasn't ready to rise when I woke up from a sweet sleep cycle at four-thirty in the morning. I wasn't prepared to rise and shine either. I had only a few hours of rest, which was problematic for someone who relishes eight hours of quality sleep every night. I hoped the dark post-midnight sky would lull me back to the satisfying slumber I longed for, but to no avail.

I sat on the side of the bed, wondering what to do with this super early wake-up call. I started to feel that there was a reason I was so alert and wide-eyed at this time. I had an assignment on the horizon. Sleep could wait. We would catch up with each other later.

I shuffled into the living room, pulled up a comfortable chair, and perched myself next to a window that gave me a clear eighteen-story overview of a tranquil Lake Michigan below.

I made a spur-of-the-moment decision to sit and wait for the sunrise. Catching a first glimpse of daybreak was like watching the grand floor-to-ceiling theater curtains raised before a live stage show. We anxiously wait for the full reveal. The prospect of something new and wonderful unfolding before our eyes.

Though patiently waiting, I considered the long list of leftover tasks I failed to complete the day before and the new growing list of assignments to be tackled later in the day.

It was a relay race in my mind, with one thought after another handed off like a baton between two runners. I have since learned that waiting for the sunrise will do that to you. It may quiet the soul or jump-start your day in complete overdrive. I preferred the former.

I decided to go back to my bedroom, not to return to bed, but to settle at my writing desk, where I still had a bird's eye view of the lakefront. The sun was no longer playing peek-a-boo. It was on full display in the splendor of its glory. The gleaming rays created sparkling white pinpoints of light on the water, which appeared to move as if dancing with the ebb and flow of the morning tide. I thought of the Bible scripture in Genesis 1:2b, "And the Spirit of God moved upon the face of the waters."

I quickly retrieved my journal from my bedside table and wrote, "I'm jotting a few ideas down, the first pages of the manuscript for a book called A Million Years."

August 4, 2018
Chicago, Illinois

CONTENTS

INTRODUCTION

When I was growing up in Washington, D.C., my father would come home from his job as an attendant in the Cloak Room on Capitol Hill and, on many warm summer evenings, take me to the neighborhood playground. I was always so excited about this father-daughter time together. Picture a five-year-old girl with three pigtails joyfully skipping down the street with her daddy, hand in hand. She gripped a brightly colored metal sand bucket with a matching shovel that gently rattled inside the pail as they made their way. That would be me. Once we got to the playground, my father would push me in the swing as high as I wanted, help me climb the short step ladder to the shiny metal slide, and then catch me with open arms at the end of my ride down. Or Daddy would let me spend time building whatever my imagination and a bucket of sand could conjure up. Playgrounds were like an enchanted wonderland of fun-loving options. I fondly remember those early evenings when I could play with blissful abandonment, not having a care in the world.

Today, I live in a community with plenty of parks and playgrounds. On frequent evening walks, I see the neighborhood parents with their children having as much fun as I did at their age.

Of course, some of the playground equipment is different, but the laughter and sheer joy of the moment remain the same.

There is something to be said about this age of innocence, filled with play dates and big dreams. Every day could be full of good times without a care in the world. These are the formative years when we experience life through rose-colored glasses, fortified by irrepressible hope. Our youthful hearts go their merry way daily, not yet ruffled by life's inevitable challenges. Then one day, we have our first experience with brokenness and disappointment. We are blindsided by a traumatic event that signals the official wake-up call from the playground to adulthood. It is a seismic paradigm shift that shakes the foundation of our lives.

We could describe it as a rude awakening, opening the emotional floodgates and taking us on a wild ride with a gamut of emotions. We begin to see the world through a wide-angle lens of disillusionment. We get lost in our random thoughts. We quickly realize that life is not always full of fun and games. Playtime is over.

We had dreams about letting the good times roll. The carefree childhood days are long gone, and we are left to wonder how we arrived at this place of seemingly irreparable brokenness, deep disappointment, and unrelenting anxiety about everything. We are lost in a spiritual wilderness.

We ultimately ask ourselves and others a simple one-word question: "*Why?*"

In times of uncertainty during a barren wilderness season, we need genuine answers to bridge the gap between the darkness trying to envelop us and the light beckoning us not to give up.

I have heard wise elderly grandmothers say, "Trouble don't last always," but there are moments when we may feel like it will never end. We have been surrounded by trouble for so long that we have lost track of time. It feels like we have dealt with one thing or another, not for days or months, but for a million years!

In the grip of fear and uncertainty, trapped in the wilderness, trouble is on a search-and-destroy mission. It is mercilessly chasing us down with one cataclysmic predicament after another. We feel like we are running for our lives and running out of time. Despair lingers over us like smoke from an extinguished fire. We must honestly admit that we urgently need help.

If we are to experience any semblance of hope beyond our ever-present crises, we need to know God has a unique master plan for each of us. It is a divine blueprint to fulfill His highest purpose for our lives. God's plan is strategic, tried, and proven, but first, we must be receptive to it.

This book has been written as a spiritual guidance tool to bring renewed hope and the essential resources to help you successfully navigate your wilderness of adversity and lack.

Each chapter of this book will help you navigate the unpredictable terrain that defines the wilderness landscape. Every lesson will give you clear insight and understanding, so your stumbling blocks will become your stepping stones. In the end, your wilderness experiences will no longer define you.

May it also serve as a healing repository for your shattered dreams and overflowing tears, and may your spirit be lifted during the dark and cloudy days of unmet expectations. May it comfort you during sleepless nights, be a companion in lonely hospital waiting rooms, and be a treasure of hope behind the prison walls, whether they are physical or spiritual.

Even though it feels like you have hopelessly struggled for a million years, let the transformative journey of a lifetime begin.

The
Starting
Point

1

"And I will bring you into the wilderness of the people, and there will I plead with you face to face."

–Ezekiel 20:35 (KJV)

In my wildest dreams, I never anticipated being lost and left searching for a way out of my own spiritual wilderness. Over the years, I have realized that life does not revolve around our desired expectations. At some point, we will have to face our wilderness season, an undefined moment when we are overwhelmed by life's most challenging obstacles and have no idea where to turn or what to do. At this juncture, we reluctantly understand that life is full of uncertainties.

The wilderness is one of them.

I'm a sentimentalist who likes to record my life's journeys. The mother lode of my reminiscing is found in decades of handwritten journals, and I mean decades. I have years of journals with covers that reflect my mood or hopes for the coming year. While shopping for each new one, I remember deliberating over each journal, earnestly inspecting the cover design and the quality of the paper before committing to the final purchase. I knew every journal would become my best friend, each one I could confide in, trusting it would shelter my hopes and dreams—and on occasion, a broken heart or two. I had to choose wisely.

As the years have gone by, I now have some extra-large, sturdy, overstuffed packing boxes filled with them, many still sealed and securely taped from various wilderness moves. Every box with bold, black magic marker writing on the top and sides says VIP, my unique shorthand for very important papers. They are precious memories holding the hopes and dreams of times past.

Every once in a while, I will go into the old, dusty storage box of journals and arbitrarily select one of them, turn to a page, and read what I wrote about that particular day. I am, more often than not amazed and filled with overwhelming gratitude to note, with 20/20 hindsight, how God has been present in every single moment on every single day of my life, on the highest mountains of great joy, and in the lowest valleys of sadness and loss. He is on every page of the chronicles of my life. I also see, as a whole, how these journals weave beautiful stories of overcoming faith.

It's been said that three major areas of our lives are often pressure points during a wilderness season. The targets are family, finances, and health. For the most part, you can pinpoint your challenges because of one or all of the above. Perhaps there was an unexpected health crisis, maybe you lost money from an investment that didn't bring the expected return, or there's been a divorce or separation. Any one of those can be a devastating setback and hinder forward progress.

In my life, a constant battle was waged in the trenches surrounding personal finances. In this ongoing struggle of good versus evil, there was always a grueling boxing match between two formidable opponents. In one corner was faith, which was the Word of God, and in the opposite corner was fear, which seemingly garnered unrelenting support for its bold and consistent pronouncements of imminent bad news.

No matter how hard I worked, I seemed to dwell in a desolate financial wilderness. There never seemed to be enough money to meet all my needs, service my debt, and be a blessing to others. I can look back now and see that, under the most trying circumstances, God was teaching me to put my faith and trust in Him in these wilderness times.

During one of my nostalgic journal scavenger hunts, I found a note I had written to God, when I was on a business trip dated December 6, 2006, at 12:45 p.m. The message was on a lined writing pad from a name-brand hotel with their letterhead but no reference to the city I was visiting. As I held it in my hands, it still had the deep crease lines that revealed that I had folded the paper in half, then in half again, until it was a two-inch by two-inch square that I could insert into my wallet.

The first paragraph was respectful and honorable, but the

second was different. The heartfelt words were an indication of my wilderness state. They leaped from the page as I revisited my writing: "*Lord, I'm tired. Tell me what to do.*"

After writing that short petition, I neatly put the note away for safekeeping during my travels. Upon arriving home, I unfolded the letter, placing it on the inside cover of that year's journal without giving it a second thought. I did not get an immediate answer from God. I went about my life without financial resolution.

The overwhelming burden of a monthly home mortgage, renting a storefront meeting space for our weekly prayer group meetings, and maintaining a production office had become unmanageable and left me needing more financial resources.

I knew something had to give.

The following year, after making that journal prayer note to God for help. I received a sense of peace about selling my house. I moved into my business office, making my home in a second-floor walk-up in a semi-converted industrial building.

My conference table, customarily reserved for creative brainstorming sessions, became my dining table. The supply closet doubled as personal storage and a place to hang my clothes.

I slept on a standard sofa six feet from my desk and three feet from the freight elevator. After work hours at night, I was the only person in the building. I put an area rug and a used thrift store coffee table in my "living room" space to give me a visual separation from the dedicated work areas. My car, accustomed to being sheltered in a nice suburban garage, spent the nights in front of the office building, subject to the unpredictability of public on-street parking and Chicago's ever-changing weather patterns.

On the weekends, the owner of the building, who worked on the third floor above me, used his space to host wedding receptions and special events. Many nights, I went to sleep with the concert-level sound of music, dancing, and revelry just above my head and the freight elevator within earshot, going up and down while loading and unloading music equipment and catering services.

At times, with the hardcore rhythm of a booming bass line, the over-the-top DJ urged everyone to get on the dance floor. The partygoers responded with wild abandonment. I was convinced the almost one-hundred-year-old building's top floor would collapse with a domino effect, leaving me in a heap of rubble. The experience was wilderness living and way beyond the bounds of my comfort zone.

I had never imagined I would be making my home base in the same place I worked every day. This was a shocking turn of events that I had not expected, but I still held on, albeit with some trepidation, that eventually, everything would work out for my good. In my heart, I knew that God wanted to teach me valuable lessons that only happen in a strange and unfamiliar place like the wilderness.

I WAS IN THE WILDERNESS

The wilderness is a place between where you have been and where God wants to eventually get you in life. It is like a "transfer station," where we are seemingly alone, struggling with heartbreak, disappointment, and hopelessness. Every day, we grasp at straws, hoping something will happen to make things right again. We worry about how to "make ends meet." We fight the good fight of faith on bended knees with a bit of wishful thinking. We pray for an answer to prayer, any prayer that lets us know God is still there.

What Does the Wilderness Look Like?

The word "wilderness" is mentioned over three hundred times in the Bible, from Genesis to Revelation. There, the wilderness was often depicted as a barren and unproductive place. There's no "welcome home" mat in the wilderness. It was filled with unknown dangers, uncertainty, and fear. It was often a place of isolation, drought, and dread. The prophet Jeremiah gives us a very descriptive account of how the Lord brought the children of Israel out of Egypt and led them through the wilderness. Notice how Scripture describes the wilderness as a place of drought and utter darkness.

"They did not ask, 'Where is the LORD, who brought us up out of the land of Egypt, and led us through the barren

wilderness, through a land of deserts and ravines, a land of drought and utter darkness, a land where no one travels and no one lives?"

(Jeremiah 2:6 NIV)

What a graphic description of what it's like to be in the wilderness! Do you sense how barren and downright scary such a place can be? Can you relate to the feelings of isolation and loneliness in this place? Do you comprehend how important it would be to keep some glimmer of hope while traversing through what Jeremiah described as "utter darkness"?

In the Old Testament, King David, a man after God's own heart (1 Samuel 13:14), chosen by God to lead Israel, experienced times in the wilderness with his band of soldiers. The Bible tells us that at one point, the people in the wilderness with him were exhausted, hungry, and thirsty. I'm sure many of us have experienced at least one out of three of those things, but how do we react in that state?

When David came to Mahanaim, Shobi, son of Nahash, from Rabbah of the Ammonites; Makir, son of Ammiel, from Lo Debar; and Barzillai, the Gileadite from Rogelim, brought bedding, bowls, and articles of pottery. They also brought wheat and barley, flour and roasted grain, beans and lentils, honey and curds, sheep, and cheese from cow's milk for David and his people to eat. For they said, "The people have become exhausted and hungry and thirsty in the wilderness." (2 Samuel 17:27–29 NIV)

If you want to talk about character formation, think about some of the people you know, including yourself. How do they interact with others when they are exhausted, hungry, or thirsty? I'm often amazed at how some of the most mild-mannered people can practically "lose their religion" when patience is nowhere to be found and they can't have their way.

Character is formed in the wilderness when we are challenged in vulnerable areas of our lives. How do we respond to the tensions we feel from the relentless pressures of life? How do we deal with utter darkness when life seems so dismal? How come God is not answering my sincere prayers for help? In search of answers, this is when our disposition will begin to inform our choices and lay the groundwork for pursuing God's highest purpose.

EMOTIONS IN THE WILDERNESS

The gamut of emotions brought on by the biblical descriptions of exhaustion, thirst, and lack in the wilderness mirrors the emotions we feel in our wilderness.

- A broken marriage or a wayward child? Hopelessness takes root.

- Working and juggling an overload of family responsibilities? Exhaustion robs us of purposefulness or joy.

- That relationship you chose to have even when you knew it was not God's best. Peace flies away.

- A medical crisis? Anxiety replaces refreshing sleep, leaving us frazzled and rattled.

- Spending choices that leave us choked with debt. Fear and shame take over.

- Problems on the job with no resolutions. Bitterness and resentment emerge.

No matter what your wilderness season looks like, these are the times we may secretly ponder whether God is really concerned about what troubles us. How can we find peace when we are stuck at the intersection of fear and hopelessness? What do we do about our runaway anxiety and exhaustion from trying to manage ourselves and others? How long must we wait for change to rescue us from this abyss?

It appears time has stood still.

We try not to break down while we wait for the breakthrough. We are sick and tired of being sick and tired. As one of my friends once said, "I've been sick and tired for so long, I don't even know what I'm sick and tired about anymore."

THE WILDERNESS SEASON FEELS
LIKE A MILLION YEARS

The dark, lonely nights in the wilderness can transition to painfully long days with no hope. Sometimes, it's an hour-by-hour existence. Uncertainty abounds as we hold our breath, anxiously waiting for the other shoe to drop or for the next bit of bad news to shatter our hearts into more broken pieces. Despondency prevails as days of anguish become weeks, months, and years. We begin to think our circumstances will never change. We are being held hostage by life, trapped between the proverbial "rock and a hard place" for what feels like a million years.

We deeply desire to get out of the wilderness.

We long for

- peace
- stability
- hope
- healing
- joy

And really, there's one more thing we want. We really long for God to show up and get us out. Or at least reveal the point of the whole wilderness experience; this is why it's not uncommon to ask these questions in the wilderness:

Why?

Where are You, God?

When are You going to show up and make things better?

This book will examine these feelings and the accompanying questions typical of the wilderness season. We'll also learn valuable lessons that can only come from our personal experiences going through the wilderness.

WE WILL DISCOVER.

1. God is with us and hasn't forgotten us.

In the deepest and darkest valley, as we wrestle with the how and why, may we know without a doubt that God has not forgotten us. He is there in the lowest valleys and at the highest, seemingly impassable mountain peaks. He is there.

2. We have traveling companions.

You will not be alone as you journey through this desolate and unproductive wilderness of doubt and fear. Many are traveling a similar path. We are all trying to find our unique place where the empty spaces in our hearts will overflow with priceless peace and joy.

3. Our character is formed, and our highest purpose is discovered.

We'll discover how this unique spiritual exploration through the wilderness can develop our character and conform us to God's highest purpose for our lives. After all, "It's not *what* you are going through; it's *how* you are going through."

CHAPTER 1 - JOURNEY POINT TO PONDER

You may feel like you have been waiting a million years for your change to come. Every journey begins with the first few tentative steps. Our character formation begins in a barren and unproductive place. Still, during our wilderness season, in times of our most significant tests, we will eventually arrive at our greatest victory.

CHAPTER 1 - GUIDE POST QUESTIONS

1. In what areas of your life do you feel like you've been stuck for a million years?
2. What feelings are you experiencing in the wilderness?
3. What is your relationship with God like in the wilderness?

The
Unexpected

2

"So God led them in a roundabout way through the wilderness toward the Red Sea"

–Exodus 13:18a (NLT)

I am a television producer by trade and have been blessed to travel the world and have some wonderfully unique experiences. On one occasion, I was on a film shoot doing a piece about boat safety. My camera crew and I were excited to be out of the bleak Midwest winter weather and working on a sailboat in warm 75-degree weather in sunny Florida. We boarded the boat with the owner, an experienced sailor, ready for a creatively fulfilling production day on the water. A light, balmy breeze caught the sails perfectly, and there was no cloud in the sky as we headed out to the Atlantic Ocean. The seas were calm. I paused and took the time to relish the moment. I quietly reflected with reverential gratitude that I could enjoy a pleasant boat ride and get paid for a beautiful day on the water.

We were all enjoying our time and talking about the filming plans when suddenly we saw a dark, ominous cloud over the horizon heading our way. I thought nothing of it. However, it couldn't have been long after the sighting when a nasty storm of rain, wind, and waves enveloped our small sailboat. Alarmingly, we began to rock from side to side like a punch-drunk boxer in the last round of a losing fight. With the force of the wind, the boat started to lean dangerously to one side. It was my side of the boat. We were battered by angry waves that seemed determined to take us under.

It had gone from a bright, sunny day on tranquil waters to a dark, stormy tempest in what felt like a matter of seconds. I thought I was going to die. How could this storm come upon us so suddenly? I felt ill-prepared to save my life. Although I wore a life jacket, I was unfamiliar with how to use it. When do I pull the tab to inflate it? What if it doesn't work? There must be ferocious sharks in the water. You name it, and probably that thought raced through my mind as I held on for dear life.

I saw the sailor wrestling with the helm, trying to gain control of the sailboat. The storm was whipping the sails like they were made of flimsy tissue paper as they surrendered to every directional whim of the unrelenting winds.

I was afraid and praying that I would not lose my life on a sailboat in the Atlantic Ocean, ironically producing a video on boat safety. My cameraman stopped filming and did the best he could to manage the sails as they continued to take a beating from the blustery wind. Our lone sailor, whom we had been filming, was in a raging battle with the wind, rain, and waves. He kept saying it was going to be alright. I kept thinking, "How much longer do we have?"

Thankfully, the storm was over in about five minutes. But as far as I was concerned, it felt like a million years.

It was a reminder that when we least expect it, our peaceful lives can suddenly be overwhelmed by the raging storms of life. In these unforeseen circumstances, our world is abruptly thrown into chaos, leaving us in the wilderness, searching for answers and praying it will be over soon.

HOW WE END UP IN THE WILDERNESS

Remember the three critical areas that are often our pressure points in challenging times. There are problems in our families and with other loved ones, a lack of financial resources, and physical, mental, and emotional health concerns. Those are the scenarios we can spotlight in looking at the root causes of the wilderness experience. Still, we must consider that there are many types of events in our lives that could place us in a desolate and barren place that are the off-shoot of family, finances, and health issues. Where will your wilderness experience fit in?

CIRCUMSTANCES BEYOND OUR CONTROL LEAD US TO THE WILDERNESS

Most of us have been or know someone who has been blindsided by an unexpected turn of events that came out of nowhere and changed the course of their lives in a matter of minutes. Like my situation in the first chapter, we are affected by circumstances beyond our control. For me, it was a financial crisis due to a lack of clients and production opportunities.

Maybe you can identify your situation on this list.

- loss of job
- divorce
- death of a loved one
- financial crisis
- unexpected health concerns
- family issues
- legal problems

Like the raging storm I was caught in with my film crew, the storm comes into our lives without warning. Our world might have turned upside down and inside out before we knew what hit us. We quickly realize we have no control over what happens to us or our loved ones. We are innocent bystanders and are now swept up in a vortex of adversity.

We might feel paralyzed by fear and anguish when circumstances occur beyond our control. In shock, we asked what just happened. We are rocked off course by the radical change. We are forced into survival mode, whether we like it or not, trying to make the best out of a horrible situation.

One of the hardest wilderness seasons happens when we suffer the consequences of someone else's unwise choices. Most of the time, it just doesn't make sense to us. Perhaps you are raising your grandchildren because of your adult child's decisions. Maybe your job had a massive layoff, and you are now unemployed without financial resources. Or you might have been stricken with an unexpected illness, and you don't have health insurance.

These circumstances leave us subject to collateral damage we can't control. We are dealing with the unintended consequences of someone else's unwise choices or personal challenges that we cannot change.

Remember, our being in the wilderness is not always our fault. These are circumstances beyond our control. God is the great Equalizer. He is standing by to help right the course and guide us through with grace and love. He understands when we face challenges due to no fault of our own. We will not have to wander for a million years in the wilderness. God knows all about it, and His timing is perfect.

THE WOMAN WHO BLED FOR TWELVE YEARS

Let's look at a story in Scripture about a woman with a health problem that lasted twelve years. Looking at her story, we'll see that while we may be in a wilderness beyond our control, God is still in control.

"And a woman was there who had been subject to bleeding for twelve years. She had suffered a great deal under the care of many doctors and had spent all she had, yet instead of getting better, she grew worse. When she heard about Jesus, she came up behind him in the crowd and touched his cloak, because she thought, "If I just touch his clothes, I will be healed." Immediately her bleeding stopped and she felt in her body that she was freed from her suffering."

(Mark 5:25–29 NIV)

This unidentified woman lived with her ailment for over a decade. In seeking relief, she visited many doctors and exhausted all her financial resources, but she never lost faith. She had encountered circumstances beyond her control and did everything she could to fix the problem but to no avail. Then one day, she had a personal encounter with Jesus. It was a divine moment. She resolved to touch His clothes, believing she would be healed. Let's continue with her story.

"At once Jesus realized that power had gone out from him. He turned around in the crowd and asked, "Who touched my clothes?"

"You see the people crowding against you," his disciples answered, "and yet you can ask, 'Who touched me?'"

But Jesus kept looking around to see who had done it. Then the woman, knowing what had happened to her, came and fell at his feet and, trembling with fear, told him the whole truth. He said to her, "Daughter, your faith has healed you. Go in peace and be freed from your suffering."

(Mark 5:30–34 NIV)

What a beautiful conclusion to this woman's journey of pain and suffering. Conceivably, she left every doctor's visit wondering why me and what's next. Perhaps, as the days turned into months, she may have felt like she had been struggling for a million years, but God's timing was perfect. The woman with the issue of blood was suffering from circumstances beyond her control. Her story could have ended with no resolution except that she had an encounter with Jesus. Perhaps we should pray for a "chance meeting" with Jesus along the way in our wilderness journey. The results will be transformative if we make the right choice.

OUR OWN CHOICES LEAD US TO THE WILDERNESS

The second way we end up in the wilderness is this: we make choices (or fail to make choices) that lead us into the wilderness.

- blatant disobedience to God
- pride and arrogance
- wrong/bad choices
- refusing correction
- stubbornness
- ignoring obvious warning signs

More challenging than being a victim of circumstances beyond our control is having to reconcile the fact that our own choices led us into the wilderness. It's a sobering moment, and it's hard to come to grips with the fact that we may have sabotaged ourselves and others.

In Scripture, the Old Testament figure named King Manasseh of Judah falls into this category.

He was a wicked idolater who wholeheartedly rejected the things of God. The Bible tells us he did much evil in the eyes of the Lord, arousing His anger (2 Chronicles 33:6 NIV). We might surmise that because he was king, he could do whatever his heart desired. He didn't have to answer to anyone, and as a result, he suffered grave consequences for his self-will and disobedience.

> *"The Lord spoke to Manasseh and his people, but they paid no attention. So the Lord brought against them the army commanders of the king of Assyria, who took Manasseh prisoner, put a hook in his nose, bound him with bronze shackles and took him to Babylon."*
>
> *(2 Chronicles 33:10–11 NIV)*

The Assyrian army stripped King Manasseh of his royal garb, leaving him without any of the imperial items associated with his monarchy. To add insult to injury, he was thrown into a dungeon. In this dark black hole, he is in distress and stripped of all his glory. Here he comes face to face with his poor choices and the high price he is now paying.

We may want to point the finger at other people and blame them for our misfortune, but to be honest, we may need to do a little more soul-searching for the real reasons we find ourselves in the wilderness. The finger of blame we have pointed at others may be pointing right back at us. There are times we have willfully disobeyed what God has asked of us. With some pride, dare we even say arrogance, we have decided to do things our way. We felt obligated only to ourselves, and now we are in the wilderness, lost and aimlessly wandering.

How many of us have left the house ignoring that still, small voice telling us to take an umbrella because it will rain? We override the direction because, well, just because, and then a few hours later, we are caught in a torrential downpour. We say to ourselves or someone else, "Something told me to bring my umbrella today." At moments like that, we can only blame ourselves for being headstrong and full of self-determination. This is a relatively harmless example, but let's think about how often we have been thrust into a situation that jeopardized our lives or those of someone we loved because of our willful actions. Our pride placed us on a balance beam between life and death because we decided to "lean to our own understanding" (Proverbs 3:5 KJV). At times like this, we only have one option: we must humble ourselves before the merciful God. We see that Manasseh ultimately did this.

> *"In his distress, he sought the favor of the Lord his God and humbled himself greatly before the God of his ancestors. And when he prayed to him, the Lord was moved by his entreaty and listened to his plea; so he brought him back to Jerusalem and to his kingdom. Then Manasseh knew that the Lord is God."*
>
> *(2 Chronicles 33:12–13 NIV)*

At this moment, we must acknowledge and take responsibility for the choices that have been detrimental to ourselves and others. Here is the pivotal point in our wilderness journey when we recognize we have been free to make our own choices but not free to choose the consequences of those choices. God is in control and patiently waits for us to find our way to Him.

Let's not stay stuck in the wilderness because of our pride or sinful choices. Scripture tells us, "Pride goes before destruction, a haughty spirit before a fall" (Proverbs 16:18 NIV). When we humble ourselves, as King Manasseh did, we can find our way out of the wilderness.

EROSION OF OUR RELATIONSHIP WITH GOD

Sometimes, we are in the wilderness not because of one blatantly sinful choice but simply because we have allowed what was once a vibrant and engaging relationship with God to slowly erode by neglecting prayer, worship, and Bible study. This slow decline in our relationship with Him isn't always so evident, particularly when everything at face value appears to be going along just fine. It is a deceptively dangerous erosion that slowly wears away our love for the things of God. In Scripture, this is called "forsaking the love you had at first."

> *"Yet I hold this against you: You have forsaken the love you had at first. Consider how far you have fallen! Repent and do the things you did at first. If you do not repent, I will come to you and remove your lampstand from its place."*
>
> *(Revelation 2:4–5 NIV)*

The idea of erosion made more sense to me when I learned about one of the lakes I live near, Chicago's beautiful Lake Michigan. It is twenty-eight miles of the most scenic stretches of man-made shoreline in any lakefront city in America. Every spring, I noticed the Chicago Park District workers slowly driving along the quiet beachfront, adding sand to the shoreline. One day, someone who knew about sand and surf explained to me what they were doing. Over the frigid winter, the strong surge of waves and brutal winds force sand to be washed out into the lake, resulting in shoreline erosion. To the naked eye, you can't detect the missing sand in most places. However, the lake would lose its beachfront beauty without the replacement sand added along the shoreline in the spring.

In the same way, our poor choices can erode our relationships. When our neglected family and friends' connections suddenly fall apart, and we find ourselves in the wilderness, we may fail to realize the erosion process didn't happen overnight. This kind of deterioration is probably the most subtle, almost undetectable, because you are going along in life thinking everything is all good, and suddenly, it seems, the rug has been pulled from under you.

Admittedly, our first reaction is akin to dismay that we or others did not see the wilderness season coming. However, if we are reflective and honest with ourselves, we can acknowledge that there were ample warning signs along the way.

Can any good come out of the wilderness when we are responsible for being there? Scripture shows us that there is purpose in the wilderness, no matter what if we acknowledge God's presence in the process.

> *"But they rebelled against me and would not listen. They did not get rid of the vile images they were obsessed with, or forsake the idols of Egypt. Then I threatened to pour out my fury on them to satisfy my anger while they were still in Egypt. But I didn't do it, for I acted to protect the honor of my name. I would not allow shame to be brought on my name among the surrounding nations who saw me reveal myself by bringing the Israelites out of Egypt. So I brought them out of Egypt and led them into the wilderness."*
>
> *(Ezekiel 20:8–10 NLT)*

God took His people out of the land of Egypt, away from the situations and circumstances that would pollute them and brought them into the wilderness. He separated them from negative influences so they would be ready to hear His plans for their lives. In this barren place with very few, if any, distractions, He would have their undivided attention.

One of my spiritual mothers used to have a prison ministry, and she would often say to many of the inmates, "You weren't just arrested; you were rescued!" She implied that even with bad choices, God could intervene to keep us from making even worse mistakes.

HOW LONG WILL YOU WANDER?

Sometimes God will do something radical, beyond our comprehension, to bring us exactly where He wants us. If there are circumstances beyond our control or self-inflicted errors in judgment, He knows how to get our attention. He may place us in the wilderness and leave us for a while to rescue us as an act of love. No matter how we end up in the wilderness, we need to answer the question posed in the Old Testament book of Jeremiah, "How long will you wander my wayward daughter? For the Lord will cause something new to happen-Israel will embrace her God" (Jeremiah 31:22 NLT).

May we respond by saying we will not roam much longer as we humbly submit ourselves to God's will and embrace His highest purpose for our lives? We will not wander directionless in the wilderness for a million years. God has incredible things in store for us!

CHAPTER 2 - JOURNEY POINT TO PONDER

If we are in the wilderness through no fault of our own, we can garner the strength to make it through as long as we trust God to lead us. If we are in the wilderness because of our poor choices, we now have an opportunity for course correction by turning to God with an open heart and mind. Both scenarios require sincere introspection and an honest assessment of our lives.

CHAPTER 2- GUIDE POST QUESTIONS

1. We've looked at two primary ways we wind up in the wilderness: circumstances beyond our control or our own choices. Which one most exemplifies your experience?
2. What are your thoughts and feelings about your wilderness journey?
3. What steps can you take to restore your relationship with God and others?

Follow
The
Guide

3

"The LORD says, 'I will guide you along the best pathway for your life. I will advise you and watch over you."

—Psalm 32:8 (NLT)

Have you ever been in a physical, spiritual, or emotional state of mind where you felt suspended between two diametrically opposed forces? Confusion reigns while you are stuck, unable to pull yourself up and out. You have nobody and nowhere to turn. Time feels like it's moving as slow as molasses. You check the calendar, anticipate a sudden change of circumstances, and wait for a rescue, but nothing happens. The days appear to turn into months, and months into a million years. Yes, it feels like you have been struggling through an endless cycle of worrisome problems for 365,250,000 days, which amounts to a million years!

When I was living in my office, as I told you about in the first chapter, there were many times I wondered when the tide would turn. I desperately wanted to move forward without the anxiety of living paycheck to paycheck. I was grateful to have a fallback position like my live-work space and was appreciative of a landlord who didn't mind me turning the office into a home base. The move would help me put my financial house in order, but I realized I would need more than a place to lay my head. I was going to need wise guidance to lead me through this kind of wilderness.

WE NEED GUIDANCE

We're going to have to acknowledge that we don't know what to do. We need the wisdom of God to lead us and extricate us from our plans. After all, we're in the wilderness because life has thrown us an unexpected curveball or possibly because we've made a wrong turn and lost our way. If we want to navigate the wilderness safely, we had better get all the guidance we can to help us in this season of our lives.

IN THE WILDERNESS, WE NEED TRAVELING COMPANIONS

Over the years, I have realized there are times I don't know what I don't know. My ignorance is especially evident when going through a wilderness season. When you have more questions than answers and more problems than money, it's best not to try to figure things out yourself. After we acknowledge our need for guidance and wise counsel, our next step is to know who to turn to for that special help. Of course, we have the eternal wisdom of the Scriptures, but God has also graced each of us with unique relationships and travel companions who will support us when the weight of the world is too much for us to carry alone.

I have been blessed to have a friend like that since childhood. She is a trusted confidante with a committed faith in Jesus Christ. She always provided insight and spiritual encouragement when I needed it most. I can trust her counsel because she will always have my best interests at heart, and a strong foundation of faith undergirds her life.

I had only known my friend Rose for about a year when my mother passed away. We were pre-teens when we first met but had become fast friends early on. I don't recollect Rose saying anything uniquely profound to me about my mother's passing since we were mere teens, and the idea of death and dying was not part of our scope of life at that age. I believe she was as shocked as I was and equally lost for words, but I do know that she was a constant presence of peace and comfort. Over the years, well into adulthood, she would call me every Mother's Day, and I knew she was checking on me without even having to say much more than hello.

I learned that friendship and wise counsel are not always about having the profound answers to life's most incomprehensible crises but simply being a presence in someone's life as a guiding light through mournful periods of darkness.

God has not called us to take this journey by ourselves; even Jesus' disciples were sent out two by two. The wilderness is not a place to go alone. It is where we need to embrace instruction and guidance from someone who can lead the way and has the knowledge to help us navigate the hills and valleys on our diverse travels.

READ THE INSTRUCTIONS

It is easy to see how one can become weary and discouraged trying to forge their way on this journey. This is especially true when we are reluctant to accept good advice and follow directions. When we are bewildered and lost in the wilderness, we need solid principles from a wise guidance counselor.

We all know the folks that don't like to read the "how-to assemble" instructions when they have to put something together. They look at the picture on the box and think, "I can do that. It seems easy enough." Then, hours later, with left-over screws and misplaced parts, the "fix-it expert" humbly admits to a resounding defeat. At that moment of reckoning, a decision, admittedly borne out of desperation, is made to follow the instructions that came with the product in the first place.

If we are going to successfully make it out of the wilderness and embrace God's highest purpose for our lives, we'll have to dive deeper into our official "how-to manual," the Bible. We must be willing to follow the instructions found in the Book. The scriptures tell us, "All scripture is inspired by God and is useful to teach us what is true and to make us realize what is wrong in our lives. It corrects us when we are wrong and teaches us to do right" (2 Timothy 3:16 NLT).

Traveling through the wilderness, often a dark place with no clear directions, requires a road map that can alert us to the unsuspecting pitfalls and the surprise detours that keep us from fulfilling God's highest purpose for our life. Long before we had GPS systems in our cars, most people would never think about starting a trip of any distance without an atlas or road map, which they kept safely ensconced in their car's glove compartment. I can remember how there was always one person in the car who had the responsibility of carefully studying the map to keep the driver on the correct interstate. Their attention went back and forth between the road ahead and the specific map indicators, alerting the driver to impending exits and the occasional construction detours. Reflecting on those road trips brought to mind what we all need to get through the wilderness seasons of our lives: a tried and tested wilderness road map and guide.

GOD'S WORD IS OUR ROAD MAP

We already know from experience that the wilderness way can be filled with treacherous steps, but we have the Word of God at our disposal. Scripture tells us, "Your word is a lamp for my feet, a light on my path" (Psalm 119:105 NIV). God's Word is a brilliant light that illuminates our dark wilderness travels, preventing us from stumbling or losing our way. This light emanates from His Word, so we must make the Scriptures our road map to take us through.

If we read and study God's Word, even "hide it in our hearts," we will find each step is secure and leading us in the right direction. It will serve as our road map through this unfamiliar terrain and bring comforting peace. God will guide us and instruct us in the way we should go if we willingly allow Him to lead us.

MOSES NEEDED A GUIDE

Moses was a great leader of Israel and certainly understood the wilderness experience. Still, while he was the "Commander in Chief" and rightfully the person "in charge," as an act of humility, he ask his brother-in-law to be a guide to escort the children of Israel through the wilderness. Moses knew he had a special assignment from God but didn't pride himself on his position or power. Moses was a humble man who asked for help.

One day Moses said to his brother-in-law, Hobab, son of Reuel the Midianite, "We are on our way to the place the Lord promised us, for he said, 'I will give it to you.' Come with us and we will treat you well, for the Lord has promised wonderful blessings for Israel!"

But Hobab replied, "No, I will not go. I must return to my own land and family."

"Please don't leave us," Moses pleaded. "You know the places in the wilderness where we should camp. Come, be our guide." (Numbers 10:29–31 NLT)

If I may take some liberty to rephrase what Moses said using twenty-first-century vocabulary, it would have sounded a little more like this: "Man, we need you to help us. We don't know what to do; we're in a bind, and the wilderness is no joke. We need your eyes (vision) for direction on how to move forward!"

Moses' plea reflected his humble and submissive spirit. He was not too big or important to ask for guidance from someone. His request shows us how wise he was by acknowledging his shortcomings and therefore rejecting one of our common downfalls: the desire to be self-reliant. By simply asking for help, Moses put himself and his people in a position to navigate unfamiliar terrain successfully. We must consider this when we are willing to ask for help; it will bless us and others.

THE LITTLE BOAT & THE BIG SHIP

I witnessed this lesson while on a cruise some years ago. We were on a huge name-brand ship that was like a small city in and of itself. I loved to stand on the balcony and watch the ships as they entered and exited the ports. On this one occasion, as we were coming into a beautiful Caribbean port, I saw a tiny boat come alongside our gigantic cruise ship. I thought it must be dangerous for such a little boat to be so close to this colossal ship. Shouldn't there be some distance separating the two of them? Then I noticed on the side of the little boat the words "Pilot Boat," but I still couldn't understand why it was so close to us.

When I arrived home, I did a little internet research. The purpose of the small Pilot Boat is to have a local waterway expert on board who knows all the crucial details of the port of call. The Pilot Boat operator knows the port of call water levels and is aware of the unique maritime challenges the large cruise ship may encounter.

While the experienced cruise captain can chart travel on the wide-open seas with state-of-the-art navigational equipment, when it comes to port navigation, he needs "the locals" on a tiny boat to go alongside his massive ship and safely guide it to the port of call.

If Moses, one of God's chosen leaders, needed a "tour" guide and the big, multi-million-dollar, high-tech cruise ships needed a tiny Pilot Boat to guide them, what about you?

We need guidance because our smooth sailing isn't always as smooth as we want it to be. We may need course corrections and advice from someone like the expert on the Pilot Boat. Someone we can trust to safely help us navigate the unfamiliar waves of fear, depression, and failure that try to overtake us.

We need to hear the voice of God and know that He is the ultimate guide. He always has our best interests at heart. He has made His instructions available in the Bible, the best how-to manual known. We can also trust that God will send the right people at the right time. Their assignment will be to show us how to get safely started on our journey out of the wilderness. Our responsibility is to listen attentively and follow specific directions. We must be receptive to God's plan for us and accept that He is now the new tour guide for our lives. We must let Him lead us. We cannot do this on our own. The goal is to leave the wilderness behind, learn from it, and live fully in His highest purpose for our lives. After all, God has the master plan for our success if we embrace His way and not our own. He's the ultimate guide.

CHAPTER 3 - JOURNEY POINT TO PONDER

You will need a guide in the wilderness, so make sure you have the right navigational expert leading you and giving specific directions to take you through it safely.

CHAPTER 3 - GUIDE POST QUESTIONS

1. Who have you depended on to be your Guide, and has that helped or hindered your wilderness progress?
2. Why is it best to have a Guide who has experience?
3. Is humility seen as a personal strength or weakness in uncertain situations?

Strange
Voices

4

"Listen to counsel and receive instructions, That you may be wise in your latter days."

—Proverbs 19:20 (NKJV)

We live in a world of non-stop information, a twenty-four-hour news cycle. We are inundated with talk shows, social media, podcasts, postings, conjectures, and the list goes on and on. Many people feel entitled to share their thoughts and opinions, whether solicited or not. Especially during our wilderness seasons, we are subjected to well-meaning folk who want to tell us what they think we should do and how to solve our problems. In this wilderness space, we are subject to a vast array of seemingly influential voices that will either hinder or help us. Whose voice will we follow? Here's how Jesus answered that question.

"I tell you the truth, anyone who sneaks over the wall of a sheepfold, rather than going through the gate, must surely be a thief and a robber! But the one who enters through the gate is the shepherd of the sheep. The gatekeeper opens the gate

for him, and the sheep recognize his voice and come to him.
He calls his own sheep by name and leads them out. After he
has gathered his own flock, he walks ahead of them, and they
follow him because they know his voice."

(John 10:1–4 NLT)

We must know the voice of the Good Shepherd because He has promised to call us by name and lead us out of the wilderness. He is our Protector, Gatekeeper, and Guide, and He knows His thoughts and plans for our lives. Our challenge is discerning the voices we listen to and follow. We must always ask what God's opinion is for us during this wilderness in our lives. His voice is the only one that matters and take note: it is not always the loudest in the room, but often the still, small voice.

Let's look at Job's story to understand why listening to God's distinct voice is critical and why His voice is the difference-maker when we are at the breaking point.

The Bible describes Job as "blameless and upright, and one that feared God, and shunned evil" (Job 1:1). He was a devoted husband and the father of ten children with substantial wealth. Lastly, Job was described as "the greatest of all the men of the east" (Job 1:3).

While Job did not have his experience in the barren and unproductive *physical* wilderness, after reading his story, we can say he certainly had a *spiritual* wilderness experience, which could rightfully be called a crisis of faith. Reflecting on the major pressure points we discussed earlier, health, finances, and family, let's examine his life a little deeper. Though an upright and devoted man, Job was challenged in each area. Let's see what we can learn from his crisis management style to help us in the wilderness.

In one day, Job experienced a lifetime of breath-taking loss and trauma. Within twenty-four hours, his three daughters and seven sons died when their house collapsed on them from a great wind "from the wilderness" (Job 1:19 NKJV). That's not all; nomadic marauders killed his servants and burned up his sheep, and then another group of bandits took all of his camels and other servants. Wait, there's more: Job would later be challenged in his body with "sore boils" from the soles of his feet to the crown of his head (Job 2:7 NKJV). It was one calamity after another. Unforeseen circumstances had touched every pressure point in his life. His family, finances, and health seemed to be killed, stolen, or destroyed within hours. Job's entire world turned upside down. Let's stop and take a break. God forbid, what would you have done if you were in Job's shoes?

Here was a man described as pious and wealthy, but none of what he had or who he was could prevent him from experiencing life's sudden and unexpected hardships. No matter your social status, whether you are a superstar celebrity, Wall Street financier, minister, school janitor, or apple-pie-baking grandmother, no one is immune to heartbreaking loss on this journey called life.

However, as we look at Job's story, we can be assured that even if circumstances have stripped us of our hopes and dreams, it's not over until God says it's over.

While Job's first few chapters could make us look for the closest off-ramp, let's be encouraged as we remember our assignment. We are making our way *through* the wilderness. We must stay the course. We cannot give up on God, no matter how dire the circumstances may appear.

We must be steadfast and recognize that our instructions moving forward must come from God. He is our Wilderness Guide, not well-intentioned friends and family. There will always be people in our lives with second opinions, but the only opinion that matters, first and foremost, is that which comes from and belongs to God. The people we know and love will not have all the answers we need because they will never fully know our story. That sovereign right is reserved for the omniscient God, as we see firsthand with Job, his wife, and then his friends.

"Then his wife said to him, 'Do you still hold fast to your integrity? Curse God and die!' But he said to her, 'You speak as one of the foolish women speaks. Shall we indeed accept good from God, and shall we not accept adversity?' In all this Job did not sin with his lips."

(Job 2:9–10 NKJV)

If that was not enough, Job also got a mouthful of opinions

from his friends. His buddies assumed they understood his state of affairs and were more than willing to contribute their assessment of his trials and tribulations.

"And so it was, after the Lord had spoken these words to Job, that the Lord said to Eliphaz the Temanite, 'My wrath is aroused against you and your two friends, for you have not spoken of Me what is right, as My servant Job has."

(Job 42:7 NKJV)

Ultimately, God had to speak to Job and give him clarity and direction during his wilderness season. It would not be the voice of his wife or his close friends. God finally brought understanding and closure to this dark chapter in Job's life. He is the God of restoration.

"I have heard of You by the hearing of the ear, but now my eye sees You. Therefore, I abhor myself, and repent in dust and ashes."

(Job 42:5–6 NKJV)

Job no longer had an intellectual knowledge of God but a deep experiential understanding of God that would help put the past behind him and embrace God's highest purpose for his life.

When Job experienced one devastating blow after another, he could have loudly protested and raged against God. But he humbled himself, giving an attentive ear to hear what God had to say to him. He did not walk away from his faith. He accepted that a greater One was at work in the affairs of his life. The sovereign God, the supreme ruler, was still in full control of the whole world. He cared about the things that concerned Job and still cares about those trials and temptations that give us sleepless nights and anxiety-filled days.

Despite all of Job's prognosticators, with their "revelatory insight," Job was alone and left with more questions than answers. Yet, as his hope could have buckled under all the burdensome pressure, we see he never gave up; he remained steadfast, and his unwavering faith rewarded him with life-changing restoration. Scripture tells us, "And the Lord restored Job's losses when he prayed for his friends. Indeed the Lord gave Job twice as much as he had before" (Job 42:10 NKJV). After getting a fresh take on his circumstances, his hour of deliverance came, and his life's trajectory returned to God's highest purpose for him and his family.

What should we do when finances, family, and health all seem under attack and our faith is rapidly dwindling away? What's our takeaway from Job's life? He experienced one catastrophe after another, enough to have resulted in losing his mind and faith, but he never released his tightly-held grip on the goodness of God. His wife and his friends all had something to say, but a time came when God had the closing statement, and that's when Job received a new perspective on his devastating situation. Today, God still has the final word. You can rest your case with Him.

During wilderness seasons, many sincerely well-meaning people will freely offer unsolicited advice and direction for you. Some will say, "If I were in your shoes," and then give you a laundry list of ideas and suggestions. They are not bad people with evil intentions, but they often will not clearly understand what God is doing in your life and how He uniquely works directly with you to bring you to His highest purpose.

For all of us going through the wilderness, where our frustrations are in overdrive and threatening to make us angry and bitter toward God, we need to remember Job's words: "Naked I came from my mother's womb, And naked shall I return there. The Lord gave, and the Lord has taken away; Blessed be the name of the Lord" (Job 1:21 NKJV).

TEMPTATIONS IN THE WILDERNESS

When we were growing up, before ride-sharing became popular, we were always told not to get into cars with strangers. If we didn't know the person, no matter how persuasive they might be with an engaging story about giving us candy or ice cream, we were taught not to go anywhere with them.

The Bible reminds us how important it is to avoid temptations during our wilderness season. Many temptations center on our appetites, things we long for, but they may not align with God's highest purpose for our lives. The temptations in the wilderness might look like this:

- engagement in illicit relationships,

- uncontrollable and wasteful spending,

- overindulgence in alcohol or food,

- unauthorized use of prescription medications,

- lying,

- cheating,

- disregarding the feelings of others,

- thinking highly of ourselves and our achievements,

- and most importantly, not making God preeminent in our lives.

The scriptures succinctly summarize these temptations as the lust of the flesh, the lust of the eyes, and the pride of life (1 John 2:16 NKJV). We cannot permit out-of-control desires to dictate our behaviors and inform our character. We must always be on guard to immediately address the temptations in our hearts and minds. The apostle James, the disciple, gives excellent advice when he instructs us to "submit ourselves to God, resist the devil, and he will flee from us" (James 4:7 NIV).

James' admonishment is a critical lifesaver to adopt at all times, particularly while going through the wilderness. There are so many distractions and seemingly great opportunities to explore when we are suffering and wandering in the barren wilderness. These are our most vulnerable times when we can experience a greater tendency to trust ourselves by leaning on our own understanding. We must diligently strive to keep the main thing the main thing. Our steps should be safeguarded with a laser focus on the Lord. The grass may look greener on the other side, but it may not be where God wants to plant us.

JESUS IN THE WILDERNESS

Most of us can relate to the "common person's" wilderness experience, but it is important to remember that Jesus Christ had a wilderness experience. The Bible tells us He was sent into the wilderness by the Spirit. Whoa! Let's stop and contemplate those words in our hearts and minds. Jesus Christ, God's only begotten Son, was led into the wilderness, a barren and desolate place, not just for a weekend. Jesus spent forty days in the wilderness in a spiritual battle. Do you believe this was part of a more excellent plan of God? And might His experience help us to comprehend God's greatest and highest purpose for our lives?

> *"Jesus, full of the Holy Spirit, left the Jordan and was led by the Spirit into the wilderness, where for forty days he was tempted by the devil. He ate nothing during those days, and at the end of them he was hungry."*
>
> *(Luke 4:1–2 NIV)*

According to Luke, a disciple of Jesus Christ and the writer of this biblical account, Jesus was full of the Holy Spirit and yet was led into the wilderness by that same Spirit, spending forty days tempted by the devil.

Earlier in our reading, we learned that we all have different "ways and means" of finding ourselves lost in the wilderness. The key is not to lament that we are in a dry and thirsty land; rather, what purpose does God have for us there? What lessons are we to learn while we spend what feels like a million years going around in circles?

Let's continue looking at Jesus in the wilderness.

"The devil said to him, 'If you are the Son of God, tell this stone to become bread."

(Luke 4:3 NIV)

Take note of these alarming words: "And the devil said to him." Satan immediately gave Jesus a proposition that would challenge His God-given assignment; this is a common tactical maneuver from the evil one. However, as we will see, for each deceptive proposal, Jesus had a definitive word to reject the appeal.

Jesus answered, "It is written: "Man shall not live on bread alone."

(Luke 4:4 NIV)

Notice that Jesus had a powerful counterattack for every tempting offer presented to Him. Each of Satan's proposals, which at face value could have appeared to be innocent and well-intended, was planned to dissuade Jesus from embracing His highest purpose.

> *"The devil led him up to a high place and showed him in an instant all the kingdoms of the world. And he said to him, "I will give you all their authority and splendor; it has been given to me, and I can give it to anyone I want to. If you worship me, it will all be yours." Jesus answered, "It is written: 'Worship the Lord your God and serve him only."*
>
> *(Luke 4:5–8 NIV)*

This is the classic example of Satan's strategy to drive us off course and keep us wandering hopelessly through the wilderness without purpose or productivity. His modus operandi, or plan of action, is to disrupt our lives with detours and distractions. He constantly entices us with people, places, and things that will hinder us from embracing God's highest purpose for our lives. Jesus, having been led into the wilderness by the Holy Spirit, was not ignorant of the evil plan set before Him. He did not hesitate to boldly respond to each "appealing" offer with the Word of God.

> *"The devil led him to Jerusalem and had him stand on the highest point of the temple. "If you are the Son of God,"he said, "throw yourself down from here. For it is written:*

"He will command his angels concerning you to guard you carefully; they will lift you up in their hands so that you will not strike your foot against a stone." Jesus answered, "It is said: 'Do not put the Lord your God to the test.'"

(Luke 4:9–12 NIV)

I used to watch a television show called *Who Wants to Be a Millionaire?* On that show, contestants had to correctly answer a series of questions to make their way up a money board, leading them to the pinnacle of success, winning a million dollars.

As a part of the show's strategy, the contestants had a couple of options if they were not confident in their answers. Their choices consisted of skipping the question, phoning a friend, or polling the audience and using their answer. It was always interesting to see how self-assured the contestants were in the early rounds with the easy questions, but their responses became more tentative as the dollar amount grew. As the questions became more challenging and the amount of money grew into the hundreds of thousands, you could see their self-confidence slowly weaken as they started to rely on others for the correct answer. Just as the contestant gathered enough courage to make a choice and commit to their "best guess" answer in the early rounds, the show host would always say, "Is that your final answer?"

In the same way, when we are in this wilderness season, we must ask ourselves: When we are bombarded with appealing options from every side, what will our final answer be? Who is a trustworthy source for advice? Whose voice has access to our hearts and minds? Will we wait to hear about our next steps from the Holy Spirit, or will we succumb to the temptations of life?

Scripture tells us, "Jesus Christ said my Kingdom is not of this world" (John 18:36). He made a clear and unequivocal choice to respond to every enticing offer of the devil with the Word of God. Will that be our final answer as well?

Jesus' wilderness experience has much to teach us. First, we must submit to the will of God, our Guide, to achieve His highest purpose for us. This means we may not always understand why we are in this lonely and unproductive environment. We must trust that God will make our wilderness experiences work out for our good when it is all said and done.

Secondly, embracing wilderness lessons means we cannot retreat to our previous ways of dealing with life's disappointments. If we are truthful, we all have certain triggers that can release an avalanche of emotions.

In times of desperate lack and loneliness, we can be dangerously tempted to turn back to bad habits that impede our progress through the wilderness. When this happens, usually at the crossroads of frustration and hopelessness, we attempt to comfort ourselves. We may turn to food, alcohol, excessive shopping, previous broken relationships, and a host of other hindrances.

These are just a few things on a mile-long list that can cause us to stumble and serve as a detriment to achieving God's highest purpose as we traverse the wilderness.

Remember, Jesus' experience in the wilderness modeled how to deal with temptations that repeatedly presented themselves to us. His way of addressing the direct offers of the enemy was to defy him with the Word of God. Time and time again, we see examples like this: "Jesus answered, 'It is written: 'Man shall not live on bread alone, but on every word that comes from the mouth of God'" (Matthew 4:4 NIV).

In moments of weakness and fear, we will have to stand on the Word of God, trusting that His powerful words will draw a line in the sand and keep us from falling prey to Satan's manipulative ways. We can also note that the devil did not try to tempt Jesus just once and move on; he kept coming back until he finally realized his efforts were futile. The enemy of our soul was resoundingly defeated by God's Word and lost the temptation battle.

Next, we read in Scripture:

"Jesus returned to Galilee in the power of the Spirit, and news about him spread through the whole countryside. He was teaching in their synagogues, and everyone praised him."
(Luke 4:14–15 NIV)

After enduring forty days in the wilderness and rejecting the devil's offer with the Word of God, Jesus came out victorious. He was led into the wilderness by the Spirit, and He returned in the power of the Spirit! During His time in the wilderness, He was not weak and defeated but fortified with God's Word and received true power from on high. Jesus Christ exemplifies what God will do when we submit to His will.

In the Old and New Testaments, the wilderness experience served as a place for tests and trials. It also was a sacred place where faith and trust in God would conform people in a way that would propel them to God's highest purpose for their lives. Could your wilderness experience reap the same for you, your family, your ministry, hopes, and dreams? You will only know as you go through and come out on the other side.

What's the collective takeaway? We listen for His voice and follow Him. He will lead us into the wilderness, keep us in the wilderness, and lead us out of the wilderness. Despite how we may feel in the wilderness, it is not an exercise in futility. I once heard a preacher say, "The wilderness is not punishment but an act of love to bring us from where we are to where we need to be."

CHAPTER 4 - JOURNEY POINT TO PONDER

The wilderness is a confusing place, with many questions and few answers. Temptations can meet us at every turn. We must make the Word of God our primary source of hope and help as we follow His voice.

CHAPTER 4 - GUIDE POST QUESTIONS

1. We know there are many strange voices in the wilderness. Are there any from your personal experiences that you need to stop listening to and put on mute?

2. What special lessons can we learn from Jesus' example of being in the wilderness?

3. What temptations do you need to respond to utilizing the Word of God?

The Wilderness As A Proving Ground

5

"He gave you manna to eat in the wilderness, something your ancestors had never known, to humble and test you so that in the end it might go well with you."

—Deuteronomy 8:16 (NIV)

When we are venturing through the deep woods of the wilderness, we begin to feel like it's been a million years with no positive resolution in sight. We often experience an array of emotions that attempt to overwhelm us. We wonder if things will ever change.

During these times, I had to work extra hard to overcome discouragement, especially when I could not see the proverbial forest for the trees. I had to rehearse God's promises to be my Provider and trust that everything would be all right, if not on that particular gloomy day, in brighter days to come.

I remember hearing a young boy preach at church one youth Sunday, and his sermon title was "It's Only a Test." The young man was still a teenager, but his insight into life's challenges was beyond the scope of his years. His message helped me understand Job's words, who, in speaking about God, said, "But he knows the way that I take; when he has tested me, I will come forth as gold" (Job 23:10 NIV). There is great consolation in knowing that it is only a test; when it's over, we will have valuable lessons to bring us to His highest purpose for our lives. As it's been said, "the journey of a thousand miles begins with the first step," so let's keep going.

REMEMBER THE WILDERNESS IS TEMPORARY

At this critical juncture, it's so important to keep in mind, first and foremost, that this is a temporary placement. We are only passing through the wilderness. We are not planning to put stakes in the ground and build a permanent homestead. Instead, this is a short-term stop, a place to take a personal inventory of our lives and evaluate our spiritual makeup. After all, it's easy to be full of faith and joy when you have everything you need and things are peacefully moving along. But what happens when we encounter those unexpected bumps in the road, the potholes of life, that bring our life plans to a screeching halt? Scripture confirms we will have bumps in the road: "We are pressed on every side by troubles, but we are not crushed. We are perplexed, but not driven to despair. We are hunted down, but never abandoned by God. We get knocked down, but we are not destroyed" (2 Corinthians 4:8–9 NLT).

We can see from those words written by the New Testament evangelist Apostle Paul that he was familiar with trouble and despair. Yet he would not be solely defined by those challenging experiences. He understood that even while entangled with problems coming from every direction, God would not abandon him. So, how can we make sense of this in our lives? Could the wilderness serve as a proving ground, a place to accurately assess our faith and learn valuable lessons to help us fulfill God's highest purpose for our lives?

THE PROVING GROUND GIVES US A TESTIMONY

In 1918, the U.S. Army established an artillery testing site in Aberdeen, Maryland, called the Aberdeen Proving Ground. It was a place to thoroughly test military equipment before it was used in combat. Almost everything we use today has been tried and tested before being released to the general public. The Federal Drug Administration (FDA) and the Federal Aviation Administration (FAA) are just two examples of governmental institutions responsible for looking out for our best interests. The FDA requires extensive research and testing of drug products before they are released for sale or public consumption. The FAA has stringent general guidelines for airline companies and the aviation business. The work that these governing bodies do is not to be taken lightly. Their evaluations and decisions are a matter of life and death, so rigorous testing and strict regulations are beyond essential, as a wrong decision could have dire consequences.

How does this apply to our tests and trials? It's been said that God has given us over seven thousand promises in the Bible. The wilderness can be a personal proving ground for any one of them.

Is He the caring and loving Father who meets all our needs? Is His grace sufficient to take us through some of the most challenging times in our lives? If we call on Him, will He really answer? The wilderness is a proving ground because we will not have a testimony without it. This is our time and space to have a close encounter with God and gain new revelation of His goodness and mercy, but first, we must navigate a gauntlet of tests and trials.

God spoke to the Israelites and speaks to us today, *"Remember how the Lord your God led you all the way in the wilderness these forty years, to humble and test you in order to know what was in your heart, whether or not you would keep his commands." (Deuteronomy 8:2 NIV).*

Remember that the wilderness is a proving ground to make us, not break us. It is not some form of punishment from a Father who doesn't love or care about you. It is, in fact, a precious gift. Our loving and caring God wants to make sure we are prepared with the knowledge and discipline to forge a lifestyle that will conform to His highest purpose for our lives.

We may not want these tests, but we need them. Why? We do not know ourselves or others as well as we think we do. We need to ultimately have our Creator give us an accurate assessment of who we really are by having us go through trials and tests to measure our walk with Him and others. I have heard people say you never know who a person is deep down inside until you see them go through the unexpected dark valleys in life—sickness, divorce, unemployment, and even the death of loved ones. Will they do so with faith or falter with bitterness and anger? It is on the proving ground the refinement process can occur, and we get an accurate measure of our strengths and weaknesses.

OUT OF OUR COMFORT ZONE

Most people are not enthusiastic test-takers, whether it's an annual physical examination, a school admissions test, or a professional licensing exam. Overcome with anxiety and fear of falling short of our expectations, we want to complete our test as quickly as possible.

Self-examination is the same way. It can feel very uncomfortable and is not something we enthusiastically embrace. However, Scripture tells us it's something we need to do: "Examine yourselves to see whether you are in the faith; test yourselves. Do you not realize that Christ Jesus is in you—unless, of course, you fail the test?" (2 Corinthians 13:5 NIV).

We aren't often challenged to look closely at who we are unless a co-worker, family member, or dear friend takes issue with our tightly held preconceived notions about ourselves. When our motives or personality quirks get called into question, we have no other option than to take a sobering look at ourselves. We may not like what we see.

Likewise, with its tests and trials, the wilderness is rarely a place we would choose for ourselves. Human nature has a unique operational default called the comfort zone. We don't want to rock the boat, so we resist self-examination that might result in effective change. As the world passes us by, we are settled in our comfort zone and left wondering why we aren't making progress.

If our lives were evaluated by a supercomputer programming system, some of us would get an error message indicating we were stuck. It might show we are in a state of shock that has rendered us motionless and afraid to take any chances or trust anyone, including God.

We have made our bed in a hideout that we think will keep us sheltered from the inevitable storms of life. So while trying to stay anchored in the comfort zone of familiarity, we are stuck and unknowingly sabotaging our futures. We are not making progress out of our wilderness because we are afraid to trust and obey God. And we may not realize that some of our most uncomfortable experiences are part of our character formation, an essential part of God's divine plan for us, so we will learn to trust Him.

In this process, to pass our tests and trials, we must be determined to face our proving ground without drawing back. If we embrace it as part of God's unique plan, we will find it reaps a long-term harvest of immeasurable benefits as He builds our faith. We will learn to trust in Him outside our comfort zone.

A MOTHER'S WILDERNESS TEST

A single mother named Hagar was raising her only son when Sarah, her "baby daddy's wife," became jealous and told her she would have to leave the family compound. Hagar was like many single mothers, trying to make the best of circumstances beyond her control. She was suddenly evicted from her home and sent into the wilderness with only bread and a bottle of water. Can you imagine how distraught Hagar must have been right there and then? She and her son were facing an uncertain future with limited resources. Like any good mother, she had to be deeply worried about how she and her only child would make it.

What would happen to her and the son she loved as they wandered in the wilderness? Have you ever been in a situation where you have been evicted from your residence, your house has been foreclosed, or you lost a job and didn't know how you would make it? Being in a hopeless situation with no help will force you to turn to God for His supernatural intervention, as Hagar did.

"And Abraham rose up early in the morning, and took bread, and a bottle of water, and gave it unto Hagar, putting it on her shoulder, and the child, and sent her away: and she departed, and wandered in the wilderness of Beersheba."

(Genesis 21:14 KJV)

Hagar was literally left to her own devices, wandering in a hot and dry wilderness with no sign of life. Eventually, the bread and water would run out. She had no options apparent to her at that moment. Dejected and without hope, the Bible tells us she placed her child under some shrubs and went away so she would not have to see the child's death. This sounds like a depressing end to her story, but it does not conclude there. This wilderness experience was not an end but a new beginning. It would no longer be the *why* but the *what* that revealed God's highest purpose for this mother and her son.

> *"And she went, and sat her down over against him a good way off, as it were a bow shot: for she said, Let me not see the death of the child. And she sat over against him, and lift up her voice, and wept. And God heard the voice of the lad; and the angel of God called to Hagar out of heaven, and said unto her, What aileth thee, Hagar? fear not; for God hath heard the voice of the lad where he is. Arise, lift up the lad, and hold him in thine hand; for I will make him a great nation."*

(Genesis 21:16–18 KJV)

While Hagar lost all hope, God had already prepared a successful rescue plan that could not fail. Hagar didn't expect that she and her son would live through these terrible circumstances, but the All-knowing God had a higher purpose for Hagar and her son, Ishmael.

When we reach the end of ourselves and our circumstances seem impossible, that's the perfect time to reflect on Psalm 46:10a (KJV), "Be still, and know that I am God." His master plan will always work, even when our hopes and dreams falter along the wayside. Let us pray that God will do for us what He did for Hagar in the wilderness.

THE PROVING GROUND WILL REFINE US

Each of us has been put here on earth for a time and a season to fulfill God's special and highest purpose for our lives. We call this divine purpose. Only God can prepare us for the work uniquely assigned to us. He does that in the time-honoring way of tests and trials on the proving grounds of life.

"For you, God, tested us; you refined us like silver. You brought us into prison and laid burdens on our backs. You let people ride over our heads; we went through fire and water, but you brought us to a place of abundance."

(Psalm 66:10–12 NIV)

We already know that the wilderness experience is an inevitable part of everyone's life journey. Yes, the tests and trials are hard and may leave us feeling discouraged, but God's intent is to make our lives fruitful, above and beyond what we could ever imagine. Whether our wilderness time is a pit stop or a prolonged journey that feels like a million years, our exit will depend on our willingness to cooperate with God. Instead of seeing it as a place with rigorous tests and trials of little value, we should embrace the experience as a Godly teaching tool. We can then gratefully accept this as a golden opportunity to take us that much closer to God's highest purpose for our lives.

CHAPTER 5 - JOURNEY POINT TO PONDER

The wilderness is God's proving ground to teach us valuable life lessons and give us the critical tools to embrace His highest purpose for our lives. In this process, to pass our tests and trials, we must be determined to face the proving ground without drawing back.

CHAPTER 5 - GUIDE POST QUESTIONS

1. What areas of your life can you identify as your proving ground?
2. How is God proving Himself to you during your wilderness journey?
3. How can your faith increase to help you pass your proving ground test?

"Did Not Finish" Is Unacceptable

6

"Let us acknowledge the Lord; let us press on to acknowledge him. As surely as the sun rises, he will appear; he will come to us like the winter rains, like the spring rains that water the earth."

–Hosea 6:3 (NIV)

Some years ago, I left a successful corporate media job to start my own production company. I thought meeting clients and growing a business could not be difficult. Little did I know—really little did I know. I was overly confident and naive, having no business acumen but solely a desire to be my own boss. It was not long before I understood that cash flow was real and translated to paying a mortgage, a car note, and having some discretionary income. Needless to say, my entrepreneurial life had more bumps in the road than expected, and I started living paycheck to paycheck.

As a believer, I was convinced this was not the life God had for me. His Word said I would be a lender and not a borrower. I was the head, not the tail. I owe no man anything but to love him. I could quote Scripture after Scripture, but clearly, there was a seismic disconnect between the Word of God and what was reflected in my bank account. I was desperate for a resolution and relief from debt-induced stress. I needed to understand why I was in such a financial predicament, particularly since I felt I had honored all of the tried-and-true biblical precepts for giving. I joyfully practiced generosity and faithfully paid my tithes and offerings.

In the search for an answer, I discovered a little neighborhood church near my office that had a daily noonday prayer meeting. During my lunch break, I made my way there as often as I could get away from my production duties. I loved this prayer meeting because it was just a small group composed mainly of the church's senior citizens who loved Jesus and believed in the power of prayer.

During one of the prayer times, a devoted and kind church deacon, Brother Hill, asked if there were any personal requests for the group to pray about for those in attendance. I sheepishly raised my hand and asked Deacon Hill and the group to pray that God would get me out of this financial bind that was causing such a strain in my life.

He listened intently and then said these words I will never forget: "Sister, we're not going to pray that God gets you out. We are going to pray that God takes you through."

You can imagine my dismay when he said, "Takes you through." I thought, "Deacon, did you hear my prayer request? I want out, not to go through." I wanted a quick fix to my financial woes. Nevertheless, they interceded for me, and I left the prayer meeting feeling unheard and misunderstood.

For weeks, I couldn't shake off his words: "We are going to pray that God takes you through." Finally, I realized Deacon Hill was a wise man who was also absolutely correct, whether I understood it or not.

Although I wanted an emergency escape route and to simply get out, I was going to have to learn perseverance. My lesson was to keep going and not give up, no matter how challenging my problems had become. That revelation was a defining wilderness moment, a gift of wisdom from a faithful praying man. Without Deacon Hill's forthrightness, I would have never absorbed one of the most important life lessons the wilderness can teach: We must go through.

Getting through the wilderness will strengthen our faith and focus beyond anything we can imagine. Scripture tells us, "Blessed is the one who perseveres under trial because, having stood the test, that person will receive the crown of life that the Lord has promised to those who love him" (James 1:12 NIV).

PERSEVERANCE: AVOIDING "DID NOT FINISH"

There is a moving video on the internet of two triathlete runners, Sian Welch and Wendy Ingraham, who were literally a few feet from finishing a grueling Ironman Hawaii triathlon.

Both runners were depleted and looked like they had given their all. However, with the end in sight, they refused to get a DNF, the runners' term for Did Not Finish. They ended up crawling their way to the finish line. If there was ever a time to believe the saying, "Where there is a will, there's a way," it is when you see these two women determined not to give up. In the wilderness, we need faith-filled determination like the two runners who refused to accept a Did Not Finish next to their names.

When I first moved to Chicago to work as a television producer, one of my early assignments was to produce the Chicago Marathon Highlights Show. I knew nothing about marathons other than a bunch of people running a long distance with a numbered bib on their t-shirts, but I learned a valuable lesson about running a full marathon.

I learned the marathon was 26.2 miles. People of all sizes and athletic abilities train to run it each year. I also discovered that as runners make their way to the twenty-mile mark, a significant accomplishment for many of them, their biggest challenge lies ahead.

At this point in the race, they have been "beating the pavement" through Chicago's scenic neighborhood routes for hours. Now runners at this time are starting to physically and psychologically experience the toll that this running has unleashed on them. Many with swollen ankles, aching backs, and weak knees battle sheer exhaustion and waning energy to complete the task they had spent months training to accomplish.

With only about six miles to finish the race, the runners encounter an imposing barrier infamously known as "the wall." The wall is a psychological barrier, a time in the race when a participant can lose the will to run any further. Runners say it's when they want to give up. They are drained of energy and exhausted physically and emotionally. It is as if the wall is saying, "You have done enough. You are not going to make it. Try again next year."

In this critical moment, the runners must dig deep into a reservoir of grit and determination. They have to adopt a mindset of resolve to continue to run. Many recognize this barrier as something to push through, knowing the longest part of the course is behind them. Their finish line is closer now than ever; they must be determined to get there, whether they walk or run the last miles of the course. These courageous marathoners have decided not to have a Did Not Finish (DNF) beside their names.

In our wilderness journey, we cannot give up now. We are closer than ever to the finish line. Each of us will be able to exit the wilderness ready to receive the fulfilled promises of our prayers, hopes, and dreams. But, if we let the weight of our trials and tribulations stop us from continuing, we will be denied our promised victory. We'll miss out on the abundant blessings that emanate from fulfilling God's highest purpose for our lives. We can't give up now. A Did Not Finish (DNF) is unacceptable. We must trust that God will strengthen us every step of the way.

BEING SURE OF GOD'S LOVE

What will help us through our wilderness journey when we hit the wall? Being sure of God's love is a requirement in the wilderness. Perhaps during some of our dark days on these lonely roads, we have felt overlooked and unloved by God. Troublesome thoughts have entered our hearts and minds to make us believe we are unlovable, and that God could never forgive us for our past transgressions and offenses. We have to remind ourselves daily, if not minute by minute, that God's love remains steady and true. We must dig into Scripture to find promises of His love and draw our strength to go through based on grace and mercy.

I am blessed whenever I read the Old Testament Psalms, especially those writings attributed to King David. It seems David, a young shepherd boy, had a unique vantage point when comprehending the depths of God's love. If you ever study the life of David, you will recognize that, just like each of us, even through his faults and failures, God never stopped loving him.

In Psalm 107, David pens heartfelt words admonishing us to acknowledge and be thankful for God's love, and not just any kind of love but that which is inexhaustible, a love that never gives up on us, no matter how we have stumbled along the way. Scripture reads, "Let them give thanks to the Lord for his unfailing love and his wonderful deeds for mankind, for he satisfies the thirsty and fills the hungry with good things" (Psalm 107:8–9 NIV). As we journey, these words are a great consolation. His love is unfailing, and in a dry and barren wilderness, He will satisfy our hunger and thirst—precisely what we need for our journey.

Why is this so important? During these rough patches, we might feel like God is no longer with us, but He is. Again, we must go back to Scripture and believe His promises, like this one: "Don't be afraid, for I am with you. Don't be discouraged, for I am your God. I will strengthen you and help you. I will hold you up with my victorious right hand" (Isaiah 41:10 NLT).

In our times of tests and trials, when we may feel like we have been running a million miles for a million years, we will inevitably experience fatigue. We can reach a point where we want to get out of the race. We will not want to go any further, but the wilderness does not have a defined off-ramp. There are no clear-cut exit signs. The only way out is to go all the way through. This is our only option if we truly desire to see our lives transformed by God. It is in the wilderness where He will meet us and teach us life's most valuable lessons. In the barren and unproductive places, He leads the way to His highest purpose for us, and we experience His unfailing love in a new and dynamic way.

SUPPORT FROM STRANGERS

In the wilderness, we'll also need others to come alongside to help us avoid the Did Not Finish (DNF) designation. One year, a dear friend of mine was in Chicago to run a marathon. He was an experienced runner, so he was no novice to the vicissitudes of such a long haul. But this particular time, as he was on the course, he just ran out of fuel. He hit the proverbial wall and was ready to give up. With so much pain and discomfort, he wasn't even trying to run at this point; just walking, putting one foot in front of the other, was progress enough. Though he was just about ready to surrender to despair, something happened on the way to getting the dreaded DNF next to his name.

A few other runners he did not know came alongside him and started encouraging him. They told him that he could make it. Like a great cloud of witnesses, they seemingly came out of nowhere to inspire him, as if to say, "You've come this far, don't give up now." They jogged with him, step by step until he found the strength to continue. He crossed the finish line, albeit with some aches and pains, carrying the sense of accomplishment that perseverance has as its own victorious reward. My friend's story beautifully illustrates our need for one another, and how even kind strangers can encourage you in the wilderness, as Scripture states, "Therefore encourage one another and build each other up, just as in fact you are doing" (I Thessalonians 5:11 NIV).

In the arduous and challenging wilderness, we may believe we are not making any progress, but it is clear we are not to give up. Admittedly, there will be moments when we are overcome by exhaustion and lackluster willpower. We will think we can't go another day; we can if we trust that we are not alone. God's love has stationed help along the course of life to encourage and lead us to the finish line.

We must remember that every step, no matter how small, brings us that much closer to God's highest purpose, but we need to travel with as little excess baggage as possible.

LET GOD CARRY OUR LOAD

I once met a man who told me about a vacation he had hiking through Spain. He walked twenty miles a day along beautiful, winding country roads that would take him up and down steep hills and valleys. He started the trip with an oversized backpack full of things he thought he needed for his journey. It included his electronic notepad, cell phone, books, camera, snacks, and so on. Somewhere along the way, he realized he was carrying way more than he needed, weighing him down. He learned those items were breaking his body and soul down. After talking to fellow travelers, he discovered that his backpack was too heavy for the journey. The rule of thumb for these walkers was to make sure their backpacks did not weigh more than ten percent of their body weight. This gentleman's bag had exceeded his weight limit, so what was he to do?

He did what we all must do when heavy burdens weigh us down. He got rid of the unnecessary items and kept only those essential to his current needs. He had to free himself from the needless items weighing him down so he could finish his trek with greater ease.

We were never made to carry the world's weight on our shoulders. We have a heavenly Father who has taken full responsibility for our complete welfare. He only asks that we give every care and concern to Him because He cares for us. The Bible tells us, "Give all your worries and cares to God, for he cares about you" (1 Peter 5:7 NLT). He will do all the heavy lifting, but we must release ourselves from the responsibility of trying to make it on our own. We freely hand over our fears and anxieties about people, places, and things to Him. We will not be weighed down with worries about our future. We put our faith in his ability to see us through every test and trial.

In the wilderness, day by day, in our times of deep trouble, we can rest in God's loving care for us. We can also find loving support from others He sends our way. It is incredible how light our heavy hearts can become when we finally hand over all our problems and concerns to Him. Only God can do the perfect work and free us from the bondage of trying to manage situations beyond our control. If we stay focused on the finish line and not our present circumstances, we can make it successfully to the end. God never starts what He does not finish. He will not leave us at the midway point and tell us to make it on our own. He is our God and our Guide through this wilderness.

CHAPTER 6 - JOURNEY POINT TO PONDER

We do not have to settle for a Did Not Finish (DNF). If we stay focused on God's loving care and concern for us, we can make it through the wilderness. He will do the heavy lifting as we let Him carry our weighty burdens.

CHAPTER 6 - GUIDE POST QUESTIONS

1. Looking over your life, how has God demonstrated His love to you?

2. What non-essential things (unforgiveness, anger, hurt) are you carrying that are weighing you down?

3. How can you encourage someone who may be ready to take a DNF, knowing that faith, focus, and determination will help them achieve God's highest purpose?

Rest Stops
In The
Wilderness

7

"I am exhausted from crying for help, my throat is parched. My eyes are swollen with weeping, waiting for my God to help me."

—Psalm 69:3 (NLT)

When we feel as though we are carrying the weight of the world, whether ongoing family issues, unresolved health concerns, or a devastating financial crisis, we can quickly become overburdened and burned out. The length of the wilderness journey, the lack of necessary resources, and the unexpected twists and turns can make us feel like we are pushing water uphill. The more we do, the less we achieve. We have accepted that there is no exit ramp out of the wilderness, and we can only get out by going through, but we are exhausted. How do we deal with fatigue? The weariness of our journey?

DAVID'S REST

Perhaps you are familiar with the Bible stories about David, the young shepherd boy who later became King of Israel and is credited with writing many of the beautiful Psalms we read and sing as part of ministry worship. In his younger days, David was responsible for guarding and guiding his sheep to rich green pastures with refreshing water springs. With a watchful eye, he marshaled them through treacherous terrain full of pitfalls and unexpected sneak attacks from dangerous predators. It was arduous, seriously exhausting hard work. David shouldered life-or-death responsibilities that made times of rest essential to his well-being. He learned through experience the value of taking necessary breaks before he became broken!

In reading one of his most familiar and well-liked writings, known as the Twenty-third Psalm, he gives us insight into how he found rest even while navigating the ups and downs of his daily assignments.

"The Lord is my shepherd; I shall not want. He makes me to lie down in green pastures; He leads me beside the still waters. He restores my soul; He leads me in the paths of righteousness For His name's sake. Yea, though I walk through the valley of the shadow of death, I will fear no evil; for You are with me; Your rod and Your staff, they comfort me. You prepare a table before me in the presence of my enemies; You anoint my head with oil; my cup runs over. Surely goodness and mercy shall follow me All the days of my life; And I will dwell in the house of the Lord Forever."

(Psalm 23 NKJV)

First, David clearly understands that he has an "Overseer," a Shepherd, the Lord God, who has responsibility for him, providing protection and provision, as David did with his own sheep. After acknowledging the "Good Shepherd," he takes us on a walking tour down a path of righteousness that leads us beside still waters and restores our souls. It is a rest invitation we must accept, as it is in the fertile green pastures that God restores our war-torn souls.

Second, whenever I read this Psalm, I am struck by the words, "He makes me lie down." I know this is true because we find it difficult to "get off the grid" to take a break and rest. Often, we are forced by extenuating circumstances, sickness, unexpected changes in family responsibilities, or just sheer exhaustion to cease all activities. From David's perspective, we see there are times God will make us rest, leading us to where He wants us to go. We need to rest, even when we don't feel like we have the time or inclination to do so. We must accept the God-kind of rest that will comfort us in our weary ways, especially on a wilderness journey.

When we are in the wilderness, so much of our strength and energy is exerted trying to keep our heads above water while sacrificially committed to ongoing obligations to help others. Work, friends, and family still need us. Do we find time in our busy schedules to rest? If we don't rest, we will become depleted and try to do everything on our own strength. Rest is how we replenish all we have given out to others. If we don't find the time to be refreshed, we become susceptible to devious traps and tricks that take advantage of our fatigue. It is one thing to take care of ourselves; it's another to be responsible for protecting and providing for others. Whether, like David, that means wrangling a ragtag group of sheep who are prone to roam or, like us, seeing about the welfare of our children, an aging parent, or dealing with an assortment of professional duties, we must acknowledge our need for rest. It must have priority in our lives.

ELIJAH'S ENCOUNTER

Our lack of rest and weariness can pull us into a negative space. When life becomes too much, we may feel we cannot escape the lingering dark clouds that hover above our heads. We are weary and longing to find the cloud's silver lining to motivate us to get out of bed and approach the dawning of daybreak with renewed hope.

One of the greatest Old Testament prophets, Elijah, was so depressed in the wilderness that he sat under a juniper tree and told God he didn't want to live anymore. Fortunately, God's highest purpose for Elijah was greater than his own vision for his life. Many times, that's part of our story as well. Read Elijah's words:

"But he himself went a day's journey into the wilderness, and came and sat down under a juniper tree: and he requested for himself that he might die; and said, It is enough; now, O Lord, take away my life; for I am not better than my fathers."

(1 Kings 19:4 KJV)

It appears that Elijah had simply had enough of life and everything it had thrown his way. He sought solitude by taking a long walk to get away from it all. It was a day's journey into the wilderness, and once he got there, he petitioned God to take his life. Elijah did not know God wasn't interested in *taking* anything away from him. He wanted to *give* him something. He wanted him to experience the kind of rest that comes from being in God's presence.

"And as he lay and slept under a juniper tree, behold, then an angel touched him, and said unto him, Arise and eat. And he looked, and, behold, there was a cake baken on the coals, and a cruse of water at his head. And he did eat and drink, and laid him down again. And the angel of the Lord came again the second time, and touched him, and said, Arise and eat; because the journey is too great for thee. And he arose, and did eat and drink, and went in the strength of that meat forty days and forty nights unto Horeb the mount of God."

(1 Kings 19:5–8 KJV)

Exhausted from the day's journey, Elijah sat down under a juniper tree and fell asleep. This makes me think about the times when we are so tired from the day's activities that we can barely keep our eyes open. As much as we had planned to watch a movie with the family, we find the movie watching us as we succumb first to drowsiness and then fully surrender to sleep itself.

Elijah was in a precarious situation. He could not go any further without much-needed rest and food. After being "fed and watered" and taking a second nap, Elijah was strong enough to proceed with his assignment. God still had work for him to do. The Scriptures show us that, now fully rested, he was able to travel forty days to his next location on the strength of that rest stop. How much more could we accomplish if we just took a break from our busy schedules and allowed God to restore us with quality sleep and nourishment? Just as the angel said to Elijah, "The journey ahead is too great for you," the same could be said for us. We have more ground to cover.

At this point, Elijah felt pretty good about how things were going. He made his way through the desert to Horeb and found accommodations so he wouldn't sleep outdoors under a tree. Oh, wait, his lodging was now a cave! Did Elijah go from the proverbial frying pan into the fire?

In the ongoing saga of "Elijah's travels and trials," the Word of the Lord comes to him with an important question: "What are you doing here, Elijah?" (1 Kings 19:9). Do you get the picture? Elijah was in a damp, dark, cavernous space where bats, hibernating animals, and an assortment of insects often make their home. It doesn't sound like a place beaming with hospitality, so how does Elijah respond to God's pointed question?

"And he said I have been very jealous for the Lord God of hosts: for the children of Israel have forsaken thy covenant,

thrown down thine altars, and slain thy prophets with the sword; and I, even I only, am left; and they seek my life, to take it away."

(1 Kings 19:10)

Elijah's feelings of despair led him to believe he was the only one going through a dark season of life. How often do we ascribe the same sentiment to our challenging circumstances? We ask the question, even now, as we journey through the wilderness: *"Why am I going through this?"* The truth is, only God knows. Perhaps God orchestrates moments of solitude to help us stop and rest so that we can clearly listen to what He is saying to us.

"And he said, Go forth, and stand upon the mount before the Lord. And, behold, the Lord passed by, and a great and strong wind rent the mountains, and brake in pieces the rocks before the Lord; but the Lord was not in the wind: and after the wind an earthquake; but the Lord was not in the earthquake: And after the earthquake a fire; but the Lord was not in the fire: and after the fire a still small voice."

(1 Kings 19:11–12 KJV)

Elijah's first meeting with the angel of the Lord was under the juniper tree while lamenting the distressing circumstances of his life. This divine encounter met his basic physical needs—food and rest—giving him the strength to continue his journey. At the next rest stop, his lodging was in a hollow mountain, where he was isolated from the world, feeling alone and slipping into darkness again. Yet, in this dismal place, Elijah would hear the voice of God and be spiritually strengthened with a resolve to continue God's highest purpose for his life. Until Elijah was wholly rested and still, he was unable to clearly discern the voice of God. Many times, this is the case for us.

Not realizing he was in a short-term crisis, Elijah was burdened by a sense of fear and failure, a potentially lethal combination. Though he was a prophet of God, it seemed he had no idea that, while in his temporary wilderness experience, God had already started a renewal work for him. It would be a divine initiative for a complete restoration, catapulting him into God's highest purpose for his life. But first, he had to rest.

Why is Elijah's story so relatable to all of us? He thought he was the only one going through something. He was looking for God in the big actions—something vast and spectacular, like a fireworks show from heaven! Yet, when God spoke to Elijah, it wasn't lights, cameras, and action. It was in a still, small voice. Elijah made it through his "dark night of the soul" because he was resting in the Lord. In the unrelenting grip of fear and trepidation, he could hear God's voice.

Are you connecting the wilderness dots? He could have easily given up and succumbed to depression and defeat, but God had a higher purpose for Elijah, as He has for you. Even if you think you have exhausted second chances and depleted everything from your "grace account" God's highest purpose for your life is progressing. On your part, you have to embrace the valuable lessons you can only learn by going through the wilderness while resting in Him.

RESTING WITH JESUS

If you have ever been on a long-distance car ride, there is nothing more refreshing than seeing the highway sign that says Rest Stop ahead at the next exit. When we get a chance to get out of the car, stretch our legs, use the facilities, and grab a bite to eat, we always feel invigorated and ready for the road ahead. God gave Elijah a rest stop, not so he could "retire" from his ministry, but so he could "re-fire" and be empowered to continue invigorated and ready to resume his highest purpose in God for years to come. Let's not resist the opportunity to rest, and, while doing so, confidently know we can trust God to handle everyone and everything else in our busy lives. We will not be leaving our full calendars and jam-packed schedules up to chance but in the hands of a faithful and trustworthy God. If you look at the word restoration, the first four letters spell Rest. If we want Him to bring restoration to the lost and broken parts of our lives, we will have to embrace the rest that comes from God.

As we see from this Scripture, Jesus acknowledges the need for rest.

"And He said to them, 'Come aside by yourselves to a deserted

place and rest a while. For there were many coming and going, and they did not even have time to eat."

(Mark 6:31 NKJV)

Where is your rest stop? Your refueling station could mean you take a day off from work for quality quiet time alone, take a long scenic drive with worship music as your background accompaniment, or book a room at a local hotel for a special personal spa retreat. The key is to carve out time for yourself with God. We must take the time to rest. It is mandatory for our spiritual and physical well-being.

Whatever we think we should be doing because it won't get done without us, we let that notion go. It can wait. When we are still and rested, we can clearly hear from God and receive the refreshing from being in His presence. Fatigue is an enemy of our mind, body, soul, and spirit. We were not made to carry heavy burdens for what feels like a million years, so why should we when there's an opportunity to rid ourselves of all of this excess baggage?

"Then Jesus said, Come to me, all of you who are weary and carry heavy burdens, and I will give you rest. Take my yoke upon you. Let me teach you, because I am humble and gentle at heart, and you will find rest for your souls. For my yoke is easy to bear, and the burden I give you is light."

(Matthew 11:28–30 NLT)

If we stay focused on the promises of God and rest in Him, we will see our burdens lifted. It may not happen overnight, but it will happen for you. He will bring His promises to fruition in His perfect time if we do not become weary and drop out. We must allow the Spirit of the Lord to refresh our hearts and minds. We must accept His rest for us.

Daily, as we trust Him, we will overcome discouragement by allowing Him to do all the heavy lifting for us. And even though we may be struggling through an unwelcome and seemingly unproductive wilderness time right now, it is a season for us to garner new strength and use it to help us continue on our journey unencumbered by weariness and fatigue. As we have a precious promise, God says, "For I have given rest to the weary and joy to the sorrowing" (Jeremiah 31:25 NLT).

CHAPTER 7 - JOURNEY POINT TO PONDER

There will be times in the wilderness when we need rest, but because we are overwhelmed by everything going on in our lives, we fail to step away and allow God to restore our souls. We must rest to receive strength to continue on our journey.

CHAPTER 7- GUIDE POST QUESTIONS

1. In what ways have you been neglecting the rest that you need?
2. How can you use your time more effectively to ensure that rest is part of your spiritual and physical make-up?
3. Find a scripture to meditate on as you prepare for bed tonight, and ask God to help you rest in Him.

Waiting
In The
Wilderness

8

"Wait on the Lord; Be of good courage, And He shall strengthen your heart; Wait, I say, on the Lord!"

—Psalm 27:14 (NKJV)

A t any age, under any circumstances, waiting is one of the hardest things we have to do. We have been raised on instant gratification, which for my generation began with drive-through fast-food service, then progressed to lightning-speed microwave meals, and now comes full circle with super-high-speed internet and instant messaging.

We are not happy campers when asked to wait at the grocery store, Department of Motor Vehicles (DMV), or even while stuck in the gridlock of rush hour traffic. We are now a collective of speed-focused individuals who want everything delivered to us in rapid-fire succession. We want an unencumbered grocery store self-checkout experience, pre-paid seamless pick-up of our morning coffee, and express self-service at the post office. We don't like to wait, period.

In the wilderness, waiting for answers to prayer, for God to reveal His purpose, or for conditions to change are all scenarios that can contribute to the wilderness feeling like a million years. We will have times when we grow impatient and frustrated and begin to or are tempted to take matters into our own hands. However, God has a better plan for our waiting. In this instance, we are not talking about *what* it means to wait on the Lord, but rather *how* we should wait on the Lord.

I'm sure you will agree that it isn't difficult to list the things that have gotten on our very last nerve when going through the wilderness.

- broken relationships that appear to be irreconcilable
- overwhelming frustration at home or on the job
- feeling like you are just going in circles
- struggling financially
- health challenges
- witnessing other people's successes and wondering when your time will come

As we do not know which way to turn, it can feel like our lives are spinning out of control. Even the most minor things seem magnified under the highly pressurized wilderness environment.

The inevitable question arises: "Why me?" The pressures of this journey in the wilderness can easily lead us to settle into a place of murmuring and complaining.

This is not how God wants us to wait. While it might seem that these two innocent habits of murmuring and complaining are ways to let off some steam and can't do much harm, Scripture tells us this isn't true. The danger in all the negativity from this mindset is the implication that God is not in control and we have lost faith in Him. However, this idea cannot be further from the truth; God knows what He is doing.

"My thoughts are nothing like your thoughts," says the Lord. "And my ways are far beyond anything you could imagine. For just as the heavens are higher than the earth, so my ways are higher than your ways and my thoughts higher than your thoughts. "The rain and snow come down from the heavens and stay on the ground to water the earth. They cause the grain to grow, producing seed for the farmer and bread for the hungry. It is the same with my word. I send it out, and it always produces fruit. It will accomplish all I want it to, and it will prosper everywhere I send it."

(Isaiah 55:8–11 NLT)

DICTATING THE RULES OF ENGAGEMENT

We add unnecessary frustration to our journey when we do not wait well. When we are impatient, and in a rush for some kind of resolution to our mounting problems, we begin to wonder if God needs a little help from us to fix our situations. We desperately want to begin to dictate the rules of engagement. This is dangerous territory to tread because when we fail to wait and seek the wisdom of God, we put ourselves and others in great jeopardy. This principle is illustrated in the Bible story of Joshua and the Gibeonites. The Gibeonites' deceitful plan is a good lesson to remind us of the adage, *"You can't judge a book by its cover."* As we'll see, the Israelites failed to seek God's wisdom and took matters into their own hands, and the consequences were disastrous.

Joshua, the great understudy and heir-apparent to Moses, was deceived by a group called the Gibeonites, who, hearing of Joshua's great military conquests, thought it better they make a league with Joshua and the children of Israel before they become their militaristic casualties. The Gibeonites cleverly devised a plan to trick Joshua and the children of Israel into believing they had traveled from a far country and now wanted to make an "honest" agreement.

"And our elders and all those living in our country said to us, 'Take provisions for your journey; go and meet them and say to them, "We are your servants; make a treaty with us." This bread of ours was warm when we packed it at home on

the day we left to come to you. But now, see how dry and moldy it is. And these wineskins that we filled were new, but see how cracked they are. And our clothes and sandals are worn out by the very long journey.' The Israelites sampled their provisions but did not inquire of the Lord."

(Joshua 9:11–14 NIV)

Joshua and the children of Israel took the Gibeonites at face value, only looking at their deceptive evidence. In Joshua's failure to ask "counsel at the mouth of the Lord," he and his leaders were ill-informed and blindly lured into making an inadvisable agreement. In the end, when the whole truth was exposed, the children of Israel were upset with the contract, but Joshua could not change the deal with the Gibeonites. Joshua's only option, his last resort, was to consign them to servitude, but the deed had been done.

At every step of the way, we need to seek the wisdom and counsel of God. We must wait on Him for answers because He alone knows the thoughts and plans He has established for His highest purpose in our lives. The inability to wait will always lead to a rush to judgment. The consequences of our impatience and reluctance to wait on God and seek His direction can lead us to make hasty decisions with detrimental long-term results.

The wisdom found in Proverbs applies here: "Trust in the Lord with all your heart and lean not on your own understanding; in all your ways submit to him, and he will make your paths straight" (Proverbs 3:5–6 NIV).

CONSEQUENCES OF FORGETTING GOD'S FAITHFULNESS

When we struggle with impatience in our wilderness experience, we risk complicating why we are already in the wilderness. We forget about God's faithfulness to us in the past. We rush to judgment at our own peril. We decide to take the seemingly good job without praying about it, we decide to marry the "love of our life" without seeking Godly counsel, or we just throw caution to the wind and do our own thing. We end up making snap judgments, and when things don't turn out as we expected, we wonder why. We failed to acknowledge His past faithfulness to us and reverted to trusting in our own counsel and not waiting on God for divine directives.

We see in Scripture, including these verses in the Psalms, that the Israelites forgot God's faithfulness: "They soon forgot His works; They did not wait for His counsel, but lusted exceedingly in the wilderness, and tested God in the desert. And He gave them their request, but sent leanness into their soul" (Psalm 106:13–15 NKJV).

Those three verses are a sad summary and show us what we don't want to do as we wait—forget God's faithfulness. The Israelites forgot what God had done for them; they did not wait for His counsel and neglected to appreciate His grace and mercy. The Bible is clear: God gave them what they requested, followed by one of the most sobering thoughts written, "But sent leanness into their soul." No doubt, as we wait, the wilderness can be a lonely place of longing. Yet we must not let it deter us from focusing on how God wants this experience to benefit us. We must know that what He wants for us is greater than what we could want for ourselves, so we cannot forget how He has blessed us in the past. As we seek the Lord in prayer, let's remember to reflect on His faithfulness and patiently wait on Him.

WAITING WELL MEANS GIVING THANKS

The Bible is full of admonitions to give thanks to God in all things. The commandment to give thanks is expressed in this verse: "In everything give thanks: for this is the will of God in Christ Jesus concerning you" (1 Thessalonians 5:18 KJV). This is not to suggest, by any stretch of the imagination, that everything that has happened to us has been good, but it's an expression of confident trust that God is Good. It's the opposite of the murmuring and complaining that characterize us when we are not waiting well.

During our waiting period, we learn that only God can untangle our complicated tapestry of fear and anxiety in these troubling wilderness times. Only He can make the bad work out for our good as we continue to express our gratitude through thanksgiving for His faithfulness to us.

Even when our insurmountable circumstances appear like pressure points collapsing all around us, we must still think about the words we speak. Do our words express encouraging and life-affirming thoughts for ourselves and others? Or conversely, have we become entrapped in resentment and hopelessness, almost drowning in a pool of negativity? The Bible says, "The tongue can bring death or life; those who love to talk will reap the consequences" (Proverbs 18:21 NLT). In our impatience and frustration, we must still speak life-giving words. If not, we risk becoming ungrateful and bitter, forgetting how faithful God has been to this point on our journey.

BENEFITS OF WAITING WELL

In a beautiful verse that is often quoted, we learn the benefits of waiting well: "But they that wait upon the Lord shall renew their strength; they shall mount up with wings as eagles; they shall run, and not be weary; and they shall walk, and not faint" (Isaiah 40:31 KJV).

When the Scripture tells us we will "mount up with wings as eagles," we can envision a majestic bird with a sharp and clear vision that allows it to see its prey on the ground from two miles away. Eagles are also known for their six to seven-foot wingspan, which allows them to soar at high altitudes by just gliding along the jet stream—those fast-moving currents of wind that circle the globe. Could God be trying to tell us something by making the analogy that we can be like the eagle? If we wait on Him without murmuring or complaining, we will be equipped to soar above the trials and tribulations of life. We gain natural and spiritual strength to continue on our wilderness journey. In patiently waiting on the Lord, He is not only renewing our strength but also enabling us to now have a "bird's eye" view of the work He will do as we embrace His highest purpose for our lives.

Let's embrace the wait, not as a cumbersome duty but with an appreciation for the lessons we are being taught by being still, resting, and listening for God's wise counsel and direction without murmuring or complaining. Even though there is a common saying that time waits for no one, we can rest assured that God's waiting room is perfectly timed for each of us.

WAITING IS NOT OUR ENEMY

As we journey through the wilderness, waiting does not have to be our enemy. It can work for us and not against us. If we are wise, we will use this time in the waiting room to rest, reflect, and recalibrate—all useful tools as we refocus on God's highest purpose for our lives.

This verse from James explains how patience works on our behalf:

"Consider it a sheer gift, friends, when tests and challenges come at you from all sides. You know that under pressure, your faith-life is forced into the open and shows its true

colors. So don't try to get out of anything prematurely. Let it do its work so you become mature and well-developed, not deficient in any way."

(James 1:2–4 MSG)

When the Bible talks about being perfect and complete, God certainly already knows we are a work in progress. Still, here the Scripture refers to being persistent or steadfast as we continue to patiently wait for God to give us His divine plan to live His highest purpose for our lives.

On one occasion, I received great advice about the valuable role time can play in our decision-making process. I met an elderly nun and engaged in a short, casual conversation about her life. I'm not sure how we got on the subject of time and the necessity of waiting, but she gave me some great advice. She told me, "Always take two weeks before you make any life-altering decision." In other words, learn to love waiting.

It sounds simplistic, but I soon came to realize that in the hustle and bustle of the world we live in, while two weeks may seem like an eternity, those fourteen days could be the difference between following His highest purpose or embarking on an unplanned detour that takes you on a circuitous route through the wilderness. The key, while we wait, is to seek God and not try to figure things out on our own. We must let Him do the heavy lifting as we acknowledge He is in charge and control. He alone knows the way that will safely lead us through our wilderness journey.

As our wise and clear-sighted Guide, God has shown us how beneficial it is to wait and let Him take the lead in managing our busy lives. In doing so, He protects us from making ill-formed decisions that could keep us stuck in the wilderness. While we have become accustomed to an express-service lifestyle, waiting is not our enemy. It teaches us to use our time wisely, be grateful for where we are, and, by faith, be thankful for where God is taking us. So let's discard negative thoughts, actions, and words so the perfect will of God can elevate us to the place He has prepared for our lives. When we arrive at our destination, we'll be able to see the immense value of patiently waiting on God and reaping the unexpected blessings and benefits of doing so.

CHAPTER 8 - JOURNEY POINT TO PONDER

While none of us like to wait, we must embrace the inherent value of doing so. When we do, we realize waiting is not our enemy but a long-suffering, gracious instructor who teaches us patience with a heart of thanksgiving, recognizing this is also a part of God's highest purpose for us.

CHAPTER 8 - GUIDE POST QUESTIONS

1. Do you struggle with waiting? If so, why is waiting so difficult?
2. What lessons have you learned about the value of waiting on God?
3. What are you still waiting for, and how can you improve your attitude about the wait?

Perspective
In The
Wilderness

9

"Set your mind on things above, not on things on the earth."

—Colossians 3:2 (NKJV)

Sometimes, when you go through continuous trials filled with trauma and drama, you can easily lose your grip on the right perspective. Think about it like this: from a reasonable distance away, looking at the silhouette of a grand mountain, it appears to be a miniature piece of rock in a vast wilderness. On the other hand, standing at the base of that same mountain and looking in awe, the crest appears impressive and impassable. Perspective is everything.

While we are waiting on the Lord to move on our behalf, so much of how we perceive the wilderness is based on our perspective as we are going through it. I like to think of perspective as something akin to a personal point of view. It can be very subjective and is often determined by the lens we are looking through. While some people may see a 12-ounce glass of water filled to the 6-ounce level as half full, someone else will see it as half empty; it's all about the perspective. Whether you are a half-full or half-empty glass person, your perspective frames how you look at life and God, Himself.

GOD'S VANTAGE POINT

Our prayer ministry rented a small storefront just south of Chicago's Magnificent Mile for years. We leased the space from an elderly gentleman who had been in the real estate business for decades. When we first met him, he was in his eighties, but his age didn't hinder him from living an active life. He came by frequently to check on his properties in the neighborhood and collect his rent payments. I didn't know much about his personal life except that his wife had passed away, and he had adult children and grandkids. However, I concluded that anyone who had lived eight-plus decades had experienced a wilderness season or two along the way.

All of us at the prayer center admired his zest for life and his upbeat spirit. When he passed away well into his nineties, I began to reflect on a very simple and valuable life lesson he unknowingly taught me about perspective.

Every time, and I do mean every time he stopped by the prayer center, I would ask, "How are you doing today?"

Not missing a beat, he would faithfully say, "Miss Beverly, I never had a bad day in my life!" I will never forget those words. I was amazed. Here was a man who had lived over nine decades, experienced the death of loved ones, encountered health issues and family challenges, and all that comes with life, and declared with unwavering conviction, "I never had a bad day in my life."

His perspective could be summed up in this Scripture:

"For our present troubles are small and won't last very long. Yet they produce for us a glory that vastly outweighs them and will last forever! So we don't look at the troubles we can see now; rather, we fix our gaze on things that cannot be seen. For the things we see now will soon be gone, but the things we cannot see will last forever."

(2 Corinthians 4:17–18 NLT)

This is a perspective, and more importantly, a panoramic view of life, that we should all wrap our hearts and minds around. His outlook was not one of denial or delusional thinking, but more of an intentional and conscious decision to see the good in life each and every day.

As we venture through the wilderness, let's find the good and cleave to it, remembering that God's vantage point is the only point of view that matters. His vantage point is summed up in this Scripture: "For I know the plans I have for you, declares the Lord, plans to prosper you and not to harm you, plans to give you hope and a future" (Jeremiah 29:11 NIV). When we recognize God as the Omniscient One, who has all knowledge, we can conclude that nothing catches Him by surprise. He is our ultimate Strategic Partner. If we humbly submit to His plans, the end result will exceed our expectations.

A minister I met some years ago had a similar perspective on life. When a conversation turned to how bad a day it was for someone, he delicately shifted the bad-day viewpoint to a different perspective. He always responded, "Well, today was a good day; tomorrow will be a better day." Again, when we frame our experiences, letting them synchronize with God's perspective on our lives, we won't allow bad days to be burdensome. Those less-than-perfect days will not determine our moods and dictate our outlook on the world.

CHANGING OUR PERSPECTIVE

Adopting God's perspective might seem easier said than done at first. No one expects this kind of outlook to change overnight, but if we approach the disappointments of the day with a determination to stop and take a deep breath, we can turn the tide of a defeatist attitude. As we gain a fresh perspective, we will see that incremental steps can make a big difference in our outlook.

Having God's perspective and seeing our lives through the lens of faith will help us get through the wilderness without succumbing to bitterness, discouragement, or even anger toward God and others. We need God's unique point of view because He sees what we can't see and knows what we don't know. He literally has the full panoramic view of your life. He knows the full scope of His divine plans for you. He asks only that we place our trust not in our resources and networking connections but in His sovereign power to execute His highest purpose in our lives. As Jesus has said, "With God all things are possible" (Matthew 19:26 NKJV). So, let's place our complete confidence in Him and allow His highest purpose to elevate us above our trying circumstances.

In this Psalm, we find a beautiful promise for each of us: "Because he has set his love upon Me, therefore I will deliver him; I will set him on high because he has known My name" (Psalm 91:14 NKJV). When we enter into a committed, loving relationship with God, He promises to be there for us and to set us above our trials and tribulations so that we can truly say we are overcomers. Indeed, we will have moments, even seasons, in our lives where so many stressful issues will try to overwhelm us, but instead of wallowing in our unfortunate state of affairs, God comes to our rescue. He will lift us above the weight of depressing defeat if we let Him. All of this is the blessed outcome of our love for Him and His love for us.

ATTITUDE AFFECTS ALTITUDE

We've heard it before, and it's true; our outlook greatly impacts our outcome, so we must guard our hearts and minds at all times.

Beverly A. Price

Here's a little aeronautical example to help us understand how our attitudes, thoughts, and behaviors can fundamentally affect our altitude or personal elevation.

First, in the interest of full disclosure, I absolutely love flying and everything associated with it. The exception is the excessive wait for luggage at baggage claim. It bears repeating for many of us that waiting isn't our strong suit, and waiting for luggage can be particularly aggravating after a long flight when you want to get home as quickly as possible.

Except for baggage claims, I love exploring airports and watching planes land and take off. I even have an app on my cell phone that allows me to listen to live air traffic control all over the world at any time. You get the picture; I'm an airplane geek.

Over the years, I have marveled at how a gigantic, fully loaded commercial jet plane with over three hundred passengers and their overstuffed luggage can rumble down an asphalt runway and lift into the air in about thirty seconds. Then, thankfully, remain airborne until it is time to land safely. During a bit of research, I learned about the critical scientific principle of aerodynamics, which is basically how planes fly. Now, please fasten your seat belt, stow your tray table, and put your seat back in the upright position. This is going to get interesting, so bear with me.

The four keys of aerodynamics are lift, weight, drag, and thrust. All four have to work in concert with one another to keep the aircraft flying at the correct speed and elevation. When a plane is airborne, there's somewhat of a give-and-take going on between lift (holding it up in the air) and weight (gravity forcing it down) and thrust (power moving it forward) and drag (slowing it down).

Now, I'm not going to make this complicated because this is the extent of my understanding of aerodynamics, but here's where we can apply these principles to our journey. When we are in the wilderness, forces will try to bring us down (weight). Still, we have to tap into the power (thrust) of God, His Word, and His promises to keep us above (lift) the self-imposed limitations and those of others that have tried to hinder and slow (drag) us from reaching His highest purpose. As we do this by constantly lifting His name and affirming our trust and faith in His promises, our outlook and attitude will change.

Subsequently, our altitude and how high we can go will also change. If we are doggedly determined not to give up, we will continue to go higher and higher until we are cruising at an altitude above life's turbulence. At times like this, it doesn't mean all of our problems will magically disappear into a jet stream, but our ability to navigate through heartache and disappointment will be markedly improved because we have a fresh way of thinking. We have put our faith and trust in God. The idea is reflected in this verse: "He sets on high those who are lowly, and those who mourn are lifted to safety" (Job 5:11 NKJV).

GOD, THE PUZZLE MAKER

Let's come in for a smooth landing and now get a ground-level perspective to help us. Have you ever seen those thousand-piece puzzles with the tiniest, oddest shapes that all seem to be the same shade of dark green? I'm sure when you saw the completed picture of the puzzle on the outside of the puzzle box, you felt confident it wouldn't be too difficult to put together. Once you started and poured all those pieces out on the table, you realized finding those first few pieces that would fit together was like looking for a needle in a haystack.

God is the puzzle maker of our lives, and He knows where you fit in, who belongs next to you, and how long it will take to complete the puzzle. If we start putting the puzzle together, as we are so inclined to do, it can become a recipe for disaster. Without the proper perspective, we will try to fit the wrong pieces into the wrong spaces. If we wholeheartedly trust God and keep His perspective, He will put the pieces together. When the big picture is complete, it will reveal His highest purpose for us.

Every personal part of us is like a distinct puzzle piece that is of the utmost importance to God. He made us in His own image. As the Puzzle Maker and as the Master Artisan, He takes each fragile piece of our broken hearts and gently places it exactly where it will fit for our good based on His divine frame of reference. It is a sacred trust making this wilderness process like a make-over for the soul. He is giving us His fresh perspective on our new life.

CHAPTER 9 - JOURNEY POINT TO PONDER

God's perspective is necessary as we journey through the wilderness because He has a unique plan for our lives. We must allow Him to rework our perspective to give us a better outlook that aligns with His highest purpose.

CHAPTER 9 - GUIDE POST QUESTIONS

1. What areas of your wilderness journey need a fresh perspective from God?
2. What have you learned about the distinct puzzle pieces of your life?
3. Why is it important to keep the proper perspective in life?

Trust And Obey In The Wilderness

10

"But blessed is the one who trusts in the Lord, whose confidence is in him."

–Jeremiah 17:7a (NIV)

Wen we tell people about putting their trust in God, it can sound relatively simple—until it's our turn to trust God in difficult circumstances. If you've been in a challenging or hurtful situation, or if you have experienced disappointment in someone or something you had previously put your confidence in, then you know that trust issues can haunt you. There is always a tinge of lingering doubt toying with your emotions that playback in your mind like a bad song stuck on repeat. These negative thoughts can produce debilitating anxiety, leaving us confused and insecure. We wonder if we'll ever be able to trust anyone again, even God.

If we are going to make it through the wilderness, we will have to determine, once and for all, to put our trust in God. We know this won't occur overnight, but it must happen if we are going to surrender every area of our lives to God and move forward. This means our dependence on others and our self-reliance have come to an end. We are placing our confidence in God. Of course, we may be tentative at the beginning, but even "baby steps" of trusting in God will help us achieve the peace we need in our lives right now. Each step will bring us closer to the full knowledge of His highest purpose for our lives.

Trust will give us confident hope that will take us through the twists and turns of the wilderness, helping us come face-to-face with our fears and disappointments. It is also where we start on a new road of recovery and discover one of the greatest blessings of all: wholeheartedly trusting in God.

"But blessed is the one who trusts in the Lord, whose confidence is in him. They will be like a tree planted by the water that sends out its roots by the stream. It does not fear when heat comes; its leaves are always green. It has no worries in a year of drought and never fails to bear fruit."

(Jeremiah 17:7–8 NIV)

It would be wonderful if we could fully live with confidence in God. We wouldn't need to worry or be fearful about our future. The Scripture we just read lets us know this is possible if we place our trust in the Lord. We will be blessed, securely planted, and fruitful because our confident expectation is in Him.

OBEDIENCE: SUBMITTING TO GOD'S WILL

Before we go too far down this path, we must access one of the major keys to unlocking the doors of opportunity on the other side of the wilderness. This key can often be overlooked because it inherently requires us to submit to a will that may not be our own. We often resist it at every turn. We frequently demand it from others, but we push back on the idea that it is required of us.

We are talking about obedience, the one word that can stop us in our tracks and prolong our stay in the wilderness. Obedience is one of those expressions that can make us cringe because it feels like we are giving up our personal agency, as if we can no longer hold on to our hopes and dreams. We become fearful that we may not have our way or be able to do our own thing. But, while we might not like the idea of obedience, if we desire to make our way through the wilderness, we must accept it as a guiding principle. We are going to have to obey God, and we are going to have to do it in a timely fashion. If we procrastinate, we risk extending our wilderness journey, which already feels like a million years.

Many times, obedience might not initially make complete sense, as this story will reveal. Years ago, I had a little retreat place along a small lake in southern Illinois. It was a perfect part-time getaway for about three seasons of the year, but in the wintertime, with sub-zero temperatures and mounds of snow, it wasn't the ideal place to spend time.

Many people who had homes along this lake were snowbirds.

They left in the winter and returned when spring had finally sprung. This also means they weatherized their homes, ensuring the pipes would not freeze. On the other hand, since I was within driving distance, I thought I could just check on the place every once in a while during the winter when it was rarely used. My only travel concerns were when the roads could be slick with a dangerous coating of black ice. This happened when a thin layer of water would freeze over the highway and turn the wintery, black roadway into something akin to an ice rink. It made for treacherous driving conditions. I had to cautiously choose my travel days for safety's sake.

One morning, I was in Chicago and had this overwhelming leading of the Holy Spirit to drive down to my place. It was a beautiful, crisp, cold winter day. The roads were clear, and I figured I could check on the place, work from there for the day, and then drive back to Chicago in the late afternoon before rush hour traffic.

Before the trip, I had not considered the weather at the lake house, which had been in a freeze-thaw cycle, with some days having temperatures above freezing and others below freezing. Unbeknownst to me, this drastic fluctuation could often lead to busted water pipes, a recipe for disaster, but this scenario never crossed my mind. I was just doing a well-being check on my property and taking advantage of a good weather day for a short road trip.

I packed my laptop and hit the road, stopping for a few snacks to sustain me until I made it back into the city for dinner. I arrived and immediately appreciated winter's serenity. The lake was frozen, the trees were barren, and there was this tranquility from the silence of winter.

I settled in and started working, taking calls, and sending emails. It was business as usual, and I felt a sense of relief that I found everything in the house and on the property as expected. A few hours passed, and I began to hear rushing water. At first, I could not determine where it was coming from, but as I checked the bathroom and kitchen, everything was fine. I proceeded outside and walked around to the side of the house. To my surprise, I saw a veritable flood of water spewing from a busted pipe. It flowed like Niagara Falls, and I had no idea how to shut it off. I feared I would soon have an unwelcome pool and then an ice skating rink in my front yard.

I made an emergency call to the local plumber; fortunately, he was in the area and could come over to my place immediately. He shut off the runaway fountain of water and fixed the problem with a special freeze-resistant valve, so I would never have that issue again.

What is the moral of the story? Going back to the beginning, if I had not obeyed the leading of the Holy Spirit to go down to the lake house on that specific day at that particular time, the pipe would have burst and I might not have known literally for weeks.

Imagine water running from your house for days in the dead of a freezing winter. Obedience and timely obedience are mission-critical. We must obey God and accept His leading by submitting to His will, not ours. Obedience will keep us out of a lot of trouble and, more importantly, bring us blessings.

"Jesus replied, 'But even more blessed are all who hear the word of God and put it into practice."

(Luke 11:28 NLT)

We can no longer just read and hear God's Word. We must put it into daily practice. Our trust and obedience must be a lifestyle decision that we adopt to bring us into His highest purpose.

COMPLETE AND UNCOMPROMISING OBEDIENCE

The children of Israel wandered in the wilderness for forty years. During that period, much of what they had to learn was centered around obedience. This would not only bring them to God's highest purpose, but it would also keep them alive as they journeyed to get there.

"The Israelites had moved about in the wilderness forty years until all the men who were of military age when they left Egypt had died, since they had not obeyed the Lord. For the

Lord had sworn to them that they would not see the land
he had solemnly promised their ancestors to give us, a land
flowing with milk and honey."

(Joshua 5:6 NIV)

We find it challenging to think that as "grown folk" people are telling us what we can and can't do. There used to be a popular chart-topping song with the lyrics, "It's your thing, do what you want to do." Every generation has adopted some kind of mantra with corresponding freedom lyrics. But if we frame this notion of obedience and freedom from a biblical perspective, we are cautioned by the experiences of the children of Israel.

What a sad commentary that an entire generation missed their highest purpose because they would not obey the voice of the Lord. This is the challenge we all face. We will soon discover that while we are free to choose, on the flip side, we are not free to choose the consequences of our choices.

We must hear the voice of God explicitly and obey it. We have to qualify explicitly because we sometimes believe that if we do a little of what God is asking of us, we are being obedient. However, the Bible does not support obedience as a partial commitment. With God, obedience is an all-or-nothing proposition. This Scripture illustrates this principle:

"But Samuel replied, "What is more pleasing to the Lord:
your burnt offerings and sacrifice or your obedience to

his voice? Listen! Obedience is better than sacrifice, and submission is better than offering the fat of rams."

(I Samuel 15:22 NLT)

When we know what God's Word tells us to do and we obey, we are positioning ourselves for His blessings. On the other hand, when we know what to do and then partially commit to it or not at all, we begin to tread on dangerous terrain. We need to be people who will listen and obey if we want to navigate safely out of the wilderness.

LEAN NOT TO OUR OWN UNDERSTANDING

Our innate human disposition makes us prone to lean on our own understanding and be wise in our own eyes (Proverbs 3:5–6 KJV). On top of being blessed with free will and the ability to make our own choices, we potentially live dangerously reckless lives unless we voluntarily submit our will and ways to God. Many of us spend way too many days, months, and years in a wilderness state because we simply refuse to let go of our stubborn and hard-fought desire to do things our way.

There was a man in the Bible by the name of Naaman. He was a respected military man who suffered from a horrible case of leprosy. A young maid who worked in his household told his wife there was a prophet, a man of God, who could heal him of his disease.

"So Naaman went with his horses and chariots and stopped at the door of Elisha's house. Elisha sent a messenger to say to him, "Go, wash yourself seven times in the Jordan, and your flesh will be restored and you will be cleansed."

(2 Kings 5:9–10 NIV)

At this point in our story, we can clearly observe how dangerous it is to lean on our own understanding. We are about to see how we can easily miss the blessings of God because they don't align with our will or what we think someone should do for us. Elisha tells Naaman to wash in the Jordan River seven times, and his flesh will be restored. What Naaman does next is a clear warning of what not to do!

"But Naaman went away angry and said, "I thought that he would surely come out to me and stand and call on the name of the Lord his God, wave his hand over the spot and cure me of my leprosy. Are not Abana and Pharpar, the rivers of Damascus, better than all the waters of Israel? Couldn't I wash in them and be cleansed?" So he turned and went off in a rage."

(2 Kings 5:11–12 NIV)

Here is a man, perhaps very much like many of us, in desperate need of help but refusing to receive it because it did not come in a manner acceptable to him. Again, our unwillingness to obey leaves us no choice but to continue in the state we are in. However, if we are willing to obey and follow the leading of the Lord, we can receive the deliverance we so desperately desire. Many times, we are called to obey in the simple matters of life. Naaman had wholesale rejected a relatively simple request. His story would have had a sadly different ending if it were not for his servants, who begged him to reconsider his headstrong, self-willed decision.

"Naaman's servants went to him and said, "My father, if the prophet had told you to do some great thing, would you not have done it? How much more, then, when he tells you, 'Wash and be cleansed'!" So he went down and dipped himself in the Jordan seven times, as the man of God had told him, and his flesh was restored and became clean like that of a young boy."

(2 Kings 5:13–14 NIV)

Naaman's story should be a call to action for us. In what areas do you need to reconsider a plan that is contrary to the will of God for your life? We could be a lot further along on our wilderness journey if we would simply decide, unequivocally, to let God's will be done in our lives. If we would accept that His will is what is best for us, we would be that much closer to grasping His highest purpose for us. Right now, while you are reading these words, faithfully and honestly declare this prayer to God from this time forward:

I ask not that my will be done, but Your will be done in my life.

It is not simply a prayer to release the self-imposed stronghold on your life but also a statement of faith. It is the confession of a powerful and unshakeable life-affirming trust in God. If you can speak those words with true conviction, you will begin to see situations change in every area of your life.

OUT OF THE WILDERNESS

Once we sincerely let go of self-will and submit to God's will, we are on our way out of the wilderness and into God's highest purpose for our lives. This is a wonderful place of liberty that will transform us. The Bible talks about Abraham, the father of faith, obediently following the voice of God even though he was not sure where he was going or what would be required of him.

"By faith Abraham, when called to go to a place he would later receive as his inheritance, obeyed and went, even though he did not know where he was going."

(Hebrews 11:8 NIV)

One of the things we can greatly appreciate about trust and obedience is what happens when we have released the bondages of self-control. When we finally embrace God's will, a lot of unnecessary weight is lifted from us.

When we have submitted every area of life to His will, we discover what God has planned for us is greater than what we ever could plan for ourselves. Scripture tells us that our thoughts are so minuscule relative to the grand plans God has for us:

"For my thoughts are not your thoughts, neither are your ways my ways," saith the Lord. "For as the heavens are higher than the earth, so are my ways higher than your ways, and my thoughts than your thoughts."

(Isaiah 55:8–9 KJV)

We are asking God for things He has already promised. We dream at ground level when He wants to elevate our vision for His highest purpose. Our trust and obedience to His perfect plans will align us with His very best for us because His ways are higher than ours.

I suspect most of us have made New Year's resolutions over the course of our lives. We begin with a grand plan to take advantage of a fresh start. We list the things that will be different for us in the coming new year. Most of the time, we would conclude that there is no harm in having an idea and then working to execute it, but doing so without God's approval can lead to unnecessary complications. Scripture warns, "In their hearts humans plan their course, but the Lord establishes their steps." (Proverbs 16:9 NIV)

Our hearts plan our course of action, as the Scripture says, but for most of us, a month or two into the new year, we have failed to accomplish much of what we intended to do. Sometimes, we are in even worse shape than before we started the new year's resolutions. How different could things turn out for us if we first sought the wisdom and direction of God, then made our list? And most importantly, in prayer, we committed ourselves to Him, trusting that He would establish the steps that led to His best for us.

The question we must seriously reflect on is this: Are we willing to trust and obey God's plan for our lives, or will we stubbornly hold on to what has already proven to be fruitless and unproductive? If we are going to stop wandering in the wilderness, we will have to concede that our plans have not worked out as expected. To get through this wilderness, we need God every step of the way.

UNEQUIVOCAL YES

If you have given Him an unequivocal *yes* to His will, don't look back. Even though it may feel like it's been a million years, you are ready to enter the final stages of preparation to leave the wilderness.

If you are still wavering and uncertain, it's understandable. No judgment, take your time but don't tarry. Your declaration of God's will in your life must be decisive and irrevocable. Saying yes to God with unwavering obedience will be life changing. No matter what problem-filled baggage is dropped at your feet, you will have a greater understanding of His unfailing love and an uncommon peace because you trust and accept His will.

There is something to be said for the soul willingly obedient to the Word of God, for the person inclined to follow God's heart, even if they do not clearly understand everything they are to do. The Bible tells us, "If you are willing and obedient, you will eat the good things of the land; but if you resist and rebel, you will be devoured by the sword. For the mouth of the Lord has spoken" (Isaiah 1:19–20 NIV). When we set out to obey Him, we increase the probability that the end results will yield a positive outcome, and we will be blessed for our trusting obedience. If we put up a fight, rebel against His instructions, and resist His direction, we risk positioning ourselves in what could only be described as a danger zone. When God asks us to obey Him, we must trust Him to guide us safely, knowing that He only wants the best for us as He leads us to His highest purpose for our lives.

As we move forward into the good land, receiving those things God has set aside for us, we must do so with confidence in Him. Our exit strategy must include prompt obedience, unshakeable faith, and a submitted will to get us to the place of His highest purpose. God has told us not to be afraid, as He describes us as a little flock. He knows our frailties and wants to watch over us if we permit Him to do so. He is a generous Father who wants to give us the kingdom, which is not just about material possessions and financial security but the things money can't buy. Jesus said, "Do not be afraid, little flock, for your Father has been pleased to give you the kingdom" (Luke 12:32 NIV). His kingdom brings healing, deliverance, peace, and many other desires that have eluded us to this point.

What a beautiful consolation as our loving Father is telling us we do not have to be overcome with anxiety and fear. He knows how far we have come and acknowledges our struggles during this wilderness journey. God reminds us that He will meet every need and lead us to His highest purpose if we trust and obey.

CHAPTER 10 - JOURNEY POINT TO PONDER

When we have submitted every area of our lives in obedience to God's direction for us, we discover what He has planned for us is greater than what we could ever plan for ourselves. We must wholeheartedly trust and obey Him as we pursue His highest purpose for our lives.

CHAPTER 10 - GUIDE POST QUESTIONS

1. Why are trust and its companion, obedience, essential in the wilderness and at all times?
2. In what areas of your life are you struggling to trust and obey God?
3. What Scriptures have you read that will help you trust God even more?

Decisions
In The
Wilderness

11

"Now listen! Today I am giving you a choice between life and death, between prosperity and disaster."

—Deuteronomy 30:15 (NLT)

I have taken some long journeys in my life, on one occasion, I traveled from my home base to the bustling city of Hong Kong. Then I followed that with a fascinating tour of the great cities of Mainland China, then to cosmopolitan Tokyo, Japan, on to the sun-drenched sandy beaches of Hawaii, and finally back home again.

As much as I lay claim to having wanderlust, a love for travel, and a desire to see the world, traveling entails a lot of detailed planning, a commitment to sticking to some kind of schedule, and, most of the time, some level of financial sacrifice. Along the way, there are bumps in the road, canceled flights, overbooked hotel rooms, and sometimes even a few health issues when our stomachs reject a delicious meal that doesn't sit right with our digestive system.

Despite the ups and downs of these journeys, I always felt that my life would be enriched by these experiences, even if I was a weary traveler and ready to sleep in my bed back home by the fifth day! With unexpected changes in the tour itinerary, challenging culinary choices, and aching feet, I didn't give up and fly back home prematurely because the itinerary didn't work out as I expected. If not for the abbreviated hotel stay in the overbooked hotel in Shanghai, I would have never taken a passenger train through the small towns of China and experienced international train travel. It was an unexpected disruption that enriched my travel there. Or who would believe that I took a Soviet-made commercial airliner from Beijing to Tokyo and there was a full-size old-school refrigerator in the rear of the coach class? Yep, grandma's refrigerator that stocked the cold drinks. Although this was many years ago, living, learning, and appreciating other people and cultures has only enriched my walk with God, which brings us to this part of our wilderness journey. Perhaps you have had a few starts and stops along the way. You may not have gone from city to city, dealing with complex trials and tribulations, trying to find God's highest purpose for your life. Maybe you picked up this book a few months ago, read a few chapters, and then life took over, but you have decided to return to it again.

What I have learned about life is that we can't straddle the fence of indecisiveness, resting on "should I or shouldn't I?" We must commit to solid decisions and then tenaciously follow through on them, no matter how the surrounding circumstances may appear. In my travels, I learned that I didn't have control over hotel arrangements, tour times, or stomach ailments. All these were part of the experience. I needed to surrender with the knowledge that it was a part of the journey. The sooner we submit to God's plan, the easier it will be to continue to fulfill His highest purpose for us.

While standing on the threshold of God's highest purpose, we are perhaps at one of the most challenging times in our journey. From here on out, we must reconcile once and for all: who will be in charge? We must be willing to give God full permission to rearrange our lives according to His highest plan for us. We can no longer be backseat drivers. If we have said, "Jesus, you are in the driver's seat," we must accept that from this point forward, our lives are in His hands. We must trust that He will make the right decisions and show us what to do. We now submit to His will and grant Him full access to every area of our lives. This will allow Him to remove any people, places, or things hindering our progress because we have consciously decided that we no longer desire to live barren and unproductive lives.

CUTTING AWAY

Moses, the great leader of Israel, was dead. He had taken his people as far as God permitted him, but not to the Promised Land. The next leader, Joshua, had the finishing work to do. He was responsible for a second generation raised in the wilderness who had not received the covenant of circumcision. If they were to proceed further, they would have to be circumcised, an expression of the cutting away of the old in preparation for the new. Scripture reads:

"So Joshua circumcised their sons—those who had grown up to take their fathers' places—for they had not been circumcised on the way to the Promised Land. After all the males had been circumcised, they rested in the camp until they were healed."

(Joshua 5:7–8 NLT)

In the same way, at this stage in our wilderness journey, God requires us to allow Him to cut away or remove any people, places, or things that will hinder our further progress. This is surgery of the heart:

"No, a real Jew is anyone whose heart is right with God. For God is not looking for those who cut their bodies in actual body circumcision, but he is looking for those with changed hearts and minds. Whoever has that kind of change in his life will get his praise from God, even if not from you."

(Romans 2:29 TLB)

Circumcision in the Old Testament represented an everlasting covenant between God, Abraham, and generations to come. Today, we understand that circumcision, the "cutting away," is not just about the flesh but, more importantly, about the heart and spirit. This is the time we submit to the "spiritual surgery" that must take place to make us whole and move us forward.

My father used to refer to surgery as "going under the knife," and just the thought of that can make many of us squeamish, but there are times when surgery is the best option to bring us healing and improve the quality of our lives.

I have known people who have needed hip or knee replacements because of an old sports injury or regular wear and tear as they aged. After a visit to an orthopedic surgeon, they had to make a critical health and quality-of-life decision. They had two options: Should they adjust their lifestyles to a new normal and live with joint pain? Or have the replacement surgery and, through modern medical technology, get a brand new knee or hip? Almost everyone opted for replacement surgery.

In some respects, this story represents where we are in the wilderness. We have faced all kinds of personal pain, lost homes, jobs, and hope. We have experienced indescribable anguish and one broken promise after another. We have had financial windfalls come and go. We cried ourselves to sleep and, in the morning, struggled to start a new day as hope felt like a distant memory. This is just a portion of what we have gone through. But now, as we come out of the wilderness, we want to make better choices so we do not repeat the same mistakes over and over again. Our new goal is to embrace God's highest purpose for our lives. In order to achieve all of this, we will need to build upon our legacy of faith and trust.

SACRED COWS

Here again is where the rubber will meet the wilderness road. We will have to let go of long-standing beliefs, attitudes, and behaviors that may have initially put us in this barren place. I called these the "sacred cows"—anything we worship and idolize above or in place of God. Here and now, He is asking for our complete devotion:

"No one can serve two masters. Either you will hate the one and love the other, or you will be devoted to the one and despise the other. You cannot serve both God and money."

(Matthew 6:24 NIV)

If what we have been through has brought us to this point and we are still unwilling to take the final steps of trust and obedience, the wilderness journey will not have been profitable for us. This is when we must throw caution to the wind and trust that God will lead and guide us if we are willing to let go of the things He asks us to release from our lives.

We are at a turning point.

We realize this can be extremely challenging. However, what if we approached it as an opportunity rather than framing it as problematic? This is the perfect time for strategic course correction in every area of our lives. No stones left unturned, and no sacred cows left standing. It is the all-or-nothing moment.

Let's start by evaluating how we invest our time, which is an excellent marker for measuring what's important in our lives. We are going to make two separate lists. On the first list, the A-List, we will note (you can number each item if you desire) how you spend your time over a typical day or week. List the top twenty things you *must* do, and feel free to add more if you desire. Consider everything you are engaged in during a typical day, such as office work, making dinner, and taking kids to sports practice.

Most importantly, take note of the amount of time you spend on all social media platforms and in conversations with friends and family, including online shopping, watching videos and television, etc.

On the opposite side of the page, make a second column. We will call it the B-List. The things you believe are essential and necessary for you to embrace God's highest purpose. It will consist of such things as morning devotions, Bible study, taking time to journal, or periods of meditation and reflection. Again, consider these activities in light of the personal relationship you want to have with God.

Now take some time away from the A-B list, pray, and come back later. It doesn't have to be the same day, but don't forget the assignment. Now evaluate the two lists.

That first list, the A-List, represents how we spend our time, money, and talent. Are we working multiple gigs so we can buy expensive status acquisitions we can't afford to impress people we may not even like? Are our relationships and time spent with family and friends helping or hurting us? Do they contribute to the greater quality of our lives in our pursuit of God's highest purpose, or do they cause us to stagnate and keep us going around in wilderness circles? Is social media defining our identity and consuming our time and attention? This is what our first list of activities will tell us about our choices, so make sure you have been completely honest with yourself. Is everything on your A-List necessary? Or are there people, places, and things that have grown around your daily schedule, like unruly weeds, that need to be uprooted to make room for something new?

The second list, the B-List, will give us some insight into the things God is nudging us to do so we can experience His highest purpose for us. How could your time, talent, and resources be better allocated so you are living out His divine plan for your life? Can most items on your second list, the B-list, be given greater priority in your daily activities? Will dropping some things from the A-List help you integrate more important lifestyle changes from the B-List? Which list will serve the greater good in your pursuit of God's highest purpose for your life?

Growing up, I enjoyed watching a TV show called *Father Knows Best*. It was about a typical suburban family with mischievous children and some interesting neighbors. No matter what the children got into, which by television standards of that era were minor mishaps, the father always had gentle, wise counsel. The show's title reminds me of our relationship with God, our Father.

He knows best, and because He is omniscient, knowing all things, we can trust His plans will always work if we let Him choose for us. Why not submit your A and B lists for His input and review, and let Him set some new priorities for your daily schedule? You might be pleasantly surprised—in a good way!

ABOVE ALL ELSE

This is the time to lay aside everything that has restrained us from moving forward. We do not have to remain stuck in a rut of frustration and defeat. We can release those things that have held us in bondage. They can no longer have the spiritual authority to hold us hostage. At this wilderness stage, we must allow the Holy Spirit to reveal every sacred cow in our lives. Remember, that's anything or anyone we give more priority and attention to than we give to God. Keep in mind that these could be people, places, or things that have unknowingly held you hostage from achieving His highest purpose for your life. God's will for us is reflected in this verse: "Seek the Kingdom of God above all else, and live righteously, and he will give you everything you need" (Matthew 6:33 NLT).

Seeking God above all else includes these steps:

- Remembering God's love
- Looking for Him to do something new
- Seeking His face

REMEMBERING GOD'S LOVE

With painful struggles and disappointments, the wilderness could have been where we lost all hope in God's highest purpose for our lives. It is the place where we could have resolved to walk away from any relationship with Jesus, concluding He was a capricious and arbitrary God who just wanted to break us down. We could have made bad decisions on top of bad decisions. However, here we are about to come out of the wilderness, not broken down but built up, not lost but found, and not conquered but as conquerors!

We must remember that "God is love" (1 John 4:16 NASB). We also have to remember, especially in hard times, that nothing will ever separate us from God's love:

"And I am convinced that nothing can ever separate us from God's love. Neither death nor life, neither angels nor demons, neither our fears for today nor our worries about tomorrow—not even the powers of hell can separate us from God's love. No power in the sky above or in the earth below—indeed, nothing in all creation will ever be able to separate us from the love of God that is revealed in Christ Jesus our Lord."

(Romans 8:38–39 NLT)

LOOKING FOR GOD TO DO SOMETHING NEW

With the assurance that nothing will ever separate us from God's love, we can eagerly look forward to the new things He has in store for us, as we see in this Scripture:

"But forget all that—it is nothing compared to what I am going to do. For I am about to do something new. See, I have already begun! Do you not see it? I will make a pathway through the wilderness. I will create rivers in the dry wasteland."

(Isaiah 43:18–19 NLT)

God continues to prove Himself, but we are struggling with the old. How can we reconcile God's new plan for us when we still feel like we have been relegated to a million years in the wilderness? Some of us may feel abandoned, angry, and resentful towards God because we feel we do not deserve what has happened to us. How can we trust that God will not let us down again? We can look back over the months and years of this wilderness journey and see that, while our circumstances may have been overwhelming, He was there with us the entire time. We were never separated from His love. No matter what, He never left, and He didn't forsake us.

SEEKING HIS FACE

If you are still anxious and wondering if God can be trusted, there's an answer in the Scriptures in God's own words.

"When I shut up the heavens so that there is no rain, or command locusts to devour the land or send a plague among my people, if my people, who are called by my name, will humble themselves and pray and seek my face and turn from their wicked ways, then I will hear from heaven, and I will forgive their sin and will heal their land. Now my eyes will be open and my ears attentive to the prayers offered in this place."

(2 Chronicles 7:13–15 NIV)

Here we see God asking some things of us: humility, prayer, turning from our corrupt ways, and, most importantly, seeking His face. Why is seeking His face important? For many of us, when we say we have been seeking God, we have mostly sought His hand. In other words, we're in a "what have you done for me lately?" relationship. We have come to Him with an extensive and well-thought-out wish list of things we want Him to do, but we forget what He wants from us. Former President John F. Kennedy said in his 1961 Inaugural Address to the nation, "Ask not what your country can do for you; ask what you can do for your country."

We could replace the word country with God and change our focus, not asking what God can do for us but, after this wilderness journey, what can we do for God?

When we seek His face, we are looking to experience an intimacy with God that is unmatched by material possessions. It becomes a relationship that truly results in the genuine knowledge of who He really is and how much He deeply loves us.

"He reached down from heaven and rescued me; he drew me out of deep waters. He rescued me from my powerful enemies, from those who hated me and were too strong for me. They attacked me at a moment when I was in distress, but the Lord supported me. He led me to a place of safety; he rescued me because he delights in me."

(Psalm 18:16–19 NLT)

ENSURE OUR HEARTS ARE NOT HARDENED

Since this is one of the last stops on the wilderness journey, we can't waste time. We have to get right with God, not by our opinion or experiences, but by doing life His way. As God has been preparing us for His highest purpose, He has one final request: be open to His love.

"Don't harden your hearts as Israel did when they rebelled, when they tested me in the wilderness. There your ancestors tested and tried my patience, even though they saw my miracles for forty years."

(Hebrews 3:8–9 NLT)

We need to make sure there are no pockets of resistance, no hidden places where our hearts are still hardened. We must remember that fear and distrust cannot usurp our blessings. God is still in control.

We can only do this by getting real with God, admitting our stubborn self-reliance, fears, doubts, disobedience, and yes, even our sins—the known and unknown places where we have fallen short of His perfect will and the highest purpose for our lives. We are all guilty as charged, so we should never feel we are being singled out for some form of cruel, unwarranted punishment. God's intent is never to harm us but to help us in the same way a loving parent would caution a young child not to touch the hot stove. The intent is to protect, not punish. Help, not harm.

As we stand on the threshold of receiving His highest purpose for us, we must remember that our hopes and dreams are not lost with God. Could it be He has a much better plan for our lives than the one we have for ourselves? He is the loving Father who decided to provide a divine blueprint for us before we ever came into the world. So it is our time to make a conclusive decision in response to His master plan. If we expect God to do something new for us, if we are truly sick and tired of being sick and tired, and if we want a deeper relationship with Him, we have no other choice but to say yes—an emphatic yes—to His will.

CHAPTER 11 - JOURNEY POINT TO PONDER

God doesn't want to lead us out of the wilderness without the tried and proven resources needed to fulfill His highest purpose. He wants us to give Him priority and trust Him to make the best choices for us.

CHAPTER 11 - GUIDE POST QUESTIONS

1. Review your personal audit of how you spend your time. What are your priorities now?
2. What challenges have you been dealing with that you need to dismiss from your life?
3. If you have said yes to the will of God, how do you expect your life to change?

Blessed
In The
Wilderness

12

"The Lord your God has blessed you in all the work of your hands. He has watched over your journey through this vast wilderness. These forty years the Lord your God has been with you, and you have not lacked anything."

—Deuteronomy 2:7 (NIV)

In the stage and film business, we often refer to the technical and creative people as the "behind-the-scenes" crew. They are not the actors on stage or in the movies, but the hard-working teams responsible for making the production happen off-stage or out of camera range. They may work in such departments as make-up, set dressing, or script supervision, to name a few. The behind-the-scenes teams provide an invaluable contribution to the creative process. Movies and television shows would not be made without their unique skill set. As audience members, we only see the polished presentation of a stage play or blockbuster movie, but behind the scenes, many key people worked to make the production a box-office success.

During our wilderness journey, God has been working behind the scenes. He is an expert at working in the background, out of public view, until the time of His big reveal. We may not have always seen His handiwork or received specific answers to our prayer requests, but there was never a moment when God was not fully aware of what was happening to us. He is the Master Architect of our lives.

At this point in our journey, we have surrendered every hope and dream to God. We have learned that an unwavering decision of wholehearted submission is a blessing. We have granted Him full rights and unabridged privileges to make whatever changes are necessary to bring restoration. We have settled, once and for all, that our devotion to Him will be one hundred percent irrevocable, a no-holds-barred commitment to His perfect will in our lives.

We are not looking back. We are focused on moving forward with faith-filled anticipation of discovering and walking in God's highest purpose for us. We have surrendered our will to His watchful care in concert with Him. We have decided that He is in the driver's seat, and we are grateful passengers along for the ride. We can trust that He knows where we need to be and that we will arrive at His planned destination on time. In the process, we have given God full permission to remove the many obstacles that have stood in our way and stifled our progress. We are cleared for the restoration process to get into full gear.

RESTORATION

During the course of this book, I have shared a few personal experiences about my various times in the wilderness. Every one of them has left an indelible imprint on my life and greatly informed my walk with the Lord. In the first chapter, I shared my story about being in a financial wilderness and selling my suburban dream home to move into my production office.

I can still remember the day I made the tough decision to let go of the suburban oasis I had lovingly called home for almost twenty years. I had gone to the office I jokingly referred to as the "international headquarters" of my one-woman production business for some weekend paperwork. As I walked up the stairs to the second-floor loft, I opened the door to the space, feeling discouraged while thinking about how I knew something would have to give. My heart felt like it was breaking, and gloom and despair wanted to overtake me. I was crestfallen and pondering my options with one big, unspoken question in the back of my mind: *how did it get to this?*

I had prayed for this specific kind of home, and God gave me everything on my prayer list: a wood-burning fireplace, check. Spacious lot and newly remodeled kitchen, check. A fruit tree in the backyard, check. If there was anything in my life that testified to God's specific answers to prayer, it was this house that I was compelled to give up.

The sweet recollections of my dream home are some of my

favorite memories about that period of my life. In the summertime, we had barbecues in the backyard, laughing and teasing one another until the sunset and the moon made an appearance. Every New Year's Eve, for as long as I owned the home, there was a special prayer meeting and celebration of the coming year. A group of us gathered and unabashedly sang our favorite gospel songs as a dear friend accompanied us on an old upright piano I had bought for such an occasion. Our songfest segued into fervent prayer as we all praised and thanked God for letting us see a new year. We then enjoyed a classic southern first-day-of-the-year culinary feast with a freshly prepared pot of black-eyed peas, collard greens, and one of Mother Dear's secret recipe pound cakes, and that's just a portion of the jaw-dropping menu. The entire time was a feast of worship, fellowship, and food. It would be late morning on the first day of the new year before some people left the all-nighter with to-go plates.

It was as if that old house had a soul of its own and would lovingly wrap its arms around us with the dogged determination not to let us go. The welcome mat was always on display, and the doors were opened to anyone who needed a temporary place to stay, a word of encouragement, or a good meal. It was everything home was meant to be.

But that particular Saturday afternoon at the production office was the moment of reckoning. It had come to the decision I had tried to avoid in my head and heart for months. I was going to have to let the dream home go. It was going to be sold.

I mourned the loss the way we do when we hear the sad news about a dear friend passing away. We take the time to cherish the precious memories. We promise never to forget their impact on our lives and the beautiful times we spent together, but we realize we must still carry on, making our way on life's journey. If I didn't want to drown in a sea of debt, overwhelmed by discouragement, I had to release the dream that had served us well for many years. And in doing so, remember that grief demands time and space but never determines the amount of time and space we give it.

The bricks and mortar would no longer belong to me, but I would have sole ownership of the remarkable memories of every prayer meeting, Bible study, and gathering we had in the little red brick bungalow. Those times became some of the defining moments of our lives, now etched in our hearts forever.

While I wanted to wallow in the loss of what I was giving up, I had so much work to do in preparation for the next steps. I could not let grief get a stronghold on me. Just like the children of Israel going through the wilderness, it was time to move when God lifted the cloud.

I checked with my landlord at the office to see if he would temporarily allow me to move into the live-work space. While I had only used it as a place of business, this would be a new rental arrangement, so I needed his approval to proceed. He was okay with it, but I could tell he wanted to make sure I would not backtrack and later complain to him about the loud music and people coming up and down the stairs on the weekends, as he often rented his space out for raucous parties and wedding receptions.

My office was actually designed as a live-work space, and though I didn't have a bedroom, there was a bathroom with a shower and a decent kitchen. I am convinced that when I rented the office years before, God knew a day would come when I would need a safe landing in the wilderness.

I had a list of things to do that felt like a mile long: find a realtor to sell my house, pack up clothes, books, and furniture, and get rid of so many things. I was downsizing to the lowest common denominator. I would only need my sofa, television, coffee table, lamp, and a few kitchen items for my new office living arrangements.

I was blessed to sell my house pretty quickly, and I used the proceeds to pay off my debts with a little left over for the down payment on the lake house. The plan was to use the place when I could not take another weekend of the landlord's special events rocking the floor above me. It would be my weekend respite, a place of solitude and relaxation.

The tide was turning in my favor. God was not going to let me drown in debt and anxiety. He sent me two life rafts. I had reliable and steady sources of income from two different clients, and I could finally see the "lighthouse" ahead. My head was above water. I had made it out of my financial wilderness with an abundance of teachable moments of reflection.

I learned that God has a unique way of answering our prayers. In His wisdom, He positions us exactly where He wants us to be to fulfill His will for our lives. He orders our steps. I had not purchased my dream home to be pressured to sell it years later; I looked at it as my life's investment, but God had a bigger plan beyond the scope of my understanding. I do not regret the circuitous way God brought me through this particular wilderness season. I still believe He blesses us to make us a blessing, even when the trying circumstances are not aligned with our hopes and dreams.

I eventually moved out of my office into a rental apartment and sold the lakefront house. It seemed again like I was following in the footsteps of the children of Israel—the cloud moved, and I moved. The lake house had sufficiently served its purpose. The memories my friends and their young children made learning to fish, going on boat rides on the neighbor's pontoon, and roasting marshmallows will always be with us. At moments like this, we are not entertaining the thoughts of what we wish we had or should have done. We are reflecting on how He kept us and are grateful beyond measure. Times like these were priceless. After moving around to five different places in as many years, God settled me in my own place, and again, He gave me the desire of my heart.

There have been many lessons to learn at each home base. The overarching message is this: sometimes God takes us through the wilderness so He can *work in us* to reveal His *highest purpose for us.* We must have faith in His promises and know He is leading and guiding us every step of the wilderness way. In my case, I had to learn, with each move from one place to the next, to trust God and confidently recognize that we always come out victoriously.

CLING TO TRUTH

Even in the restoration process, we may experience some hard things. That's just part of being alive on this side of heaven. But we have learned to look at our experiences through the lens of the promises and faithfulness of God.

Here are some Scriptures to write down, display, and memorize to remind us of these truths. As we reflect on these Scriptures, note how the writers acknowledge the difficult things they have gone through. They use descriptive words such as hardship, suffering, and loss. We might use those exact words to chronicle our own wilderness journeys, but these writers did not let those words have the final say about their lives. Yes, just like them, we acknowledge that we had to trek through dangerously challenging circumstances. However, we've learned that when we trust what God has said about us, we regain our confidence and faith in Him to successfully bring us all the way out.

Each writer moves on from the "worst of times" to better things on the horizon. We see God's restoration bringing new life, strength, blessings, and thanksgiving. Those are exactly the promises that God made to us. No matter what we have lost, no matter how broken we have been or how much despair we have experienced, we find hope in these powerful Scriptures. God is the Restorer of all things. We can trust Him to bring full restoration to every area of our lives.

"And the Lord will bless Israel again, and make her deserts blossom; her barren wilderness will become as beautiful as the Garden of Eden. Joy and gladness will be found there, thanksgiving and lovely songs."

(Isaiah 51:3 TLB)

"You have allowed me to suffer much hardship, but you will restore me to life again and lift me up from the depths of the earth."

(Psalm 71:20 NLT)

"In his kindness God called you to share in his eternal glory by means of Christ Jesus. So after you have suffered a little while, he will restore, support, and strengthen you, and he will place you on a firm foundation."

(1 Peter 5:10 NIV)

"The Lord says, 'I will give you back what you lost to the swarming locusts, the hopping locusts, the stripping locusts, and the cutting locusts. It was I who sent this great destroying

army against you. Once again you will have all the food you want, and you will praise the Lord your God, who does these miracles for you. Never again will my people be disgraced."

(Joel 2:26 NLT)

"The Lord your God has blessed you in all the work of your hands. He has watched over your journey through this vast wilderness. These forty years the Lord your God has been with you, and you have not lacked anything."

(Deuteronomy 2:7 NIV)

Each one of these Scriptures deserves time for study and meditation. They are tried and true promises to remind us that the Lord is a God who specializes in divine restoration. We know that when He restores anything in our lives, His handiwork makes it better. God does not do shabby work; we can count on His restoration to be full and complete.

LESSONS IN RESTORATION

After coming this far, we are now ready to reap the benefits of our dedication to the journey. A huge part of the restoration process is looking for and naming the blessings of the wilderness journey. As you read my lessons, consider if you have been blessed in the same ways. You might want to journal some of your revelations.

GOD WILL COMPLETE THE WORK
HE HAS STARTED

"... being confident of this very thing, that He who has begun a good work in you will complete it until the day of Jesus Christ."

(Philippians 1:6 NKJV)

There are times we feel like God has abandoned us. He gave us a plan and even answered our prayers, but now He is nowhere to be found while we are alone in the trenches battling confusion and fear. Here we are reminded that He will complete the work He started, so we should have confidence in His plan of action. We must have the courage of our convictions, trusting that God will keep His Word. If He starts something, He will finish it.

GOD IS ALWAYS WORKING

"Clearly, you are a God who works behind the scenes, God of Israel, Savior God."

(Isaiah 45:15 MSG)

Working behind the scenes does not mean that you don't have influence and impact. I already shared how there is an illustrious industry of creative professionals who work behind the scenes, and nothing would happen without their technical expertise. God is working behind the scenes on your behalf. So even if we can't see the results at this very moment, we have, by faith, the assurance that He is in control. Indeed, nothing happens without the divine input and direction of the sovereign God.

WE CAN MOVE BEYOND FAITH TO TRUST

During my wilderness journey, I had an epiphany I will never forget. I heard in my spirit these words: "You have faith, but you do not trust God." For a moment—well, actually more than a moment—I did not understand the premise. I thought faith and trust were casually interchangeable. As I contemplated the distinction, I realized there is a difference, but what is it? Here is one of my most profound life lessons:

Faith is knowing God can do something. Trust is knowing God will do it.

Does this speak to you?

I knew plenty of Scriptures that spoke to the meaning of faith, but I did not fully trust that God would do it for me. Of course, He answered many prayers in the Bible, but would He do the same for me? The answer is yes. He answered for me, and He will answer for you. But we must commit to letting faith and trust work hand in hand with us.

Do you really have faith in Him, and can you trust God with all of your heart, soul, mind, and body?

There are ample Bible stories where men and women were

challenged to have absolute faith and trust in God. The defining story of Abraham describes him as a man who was fully persuaded that what God had promised, He was also able to perform (Romans 4:21 KJV).

Mary, the mother of Jesus, had an angelic visitation and received an amazing prophecy that she would be the mother of the Messiah. Upon these words spoken to her, the Bible says she initially responded by saying to the angel, "How shall this be, seeing I know not a man?" (Luke 1:34 KJV) However, while pondering in her heart the astonishing idea that she had been chosen for such a divine assignment, she made a resounding statement of faith, saying, "Behold the handmaid of the Lord; be it unto me according to thy word" (Luke 1:38 KJV).

Let's be people who respond to God in the same way. Lord, be it unto us according to Your Word!

THROUGH PAIN AND SUFFERING, WE GET TO KNOW GOD IN A NEW WAY

Truth be told, we often get to know God for ourselves through the crucible of pain and suffering. When we have lost almost everything and He shows up at our lowest moment to tell us He will bring restoration, it is at that time that our eyes are opened and we recognize that He is the Lord God. Could this be one of the key reasons we have these wilderness experiences? To personally know God for ourselves, the One who comforts and restores as He leads us to His highest purpose? No one who has a close encounter with God ever remains the same. We know that whatever has been broken, He has the power to make whole again.

DWELLING ON THE PAST WILL HINDER OUR FORWARD MOMENTUM

"Forget the former things; do not dwell on the past. See, I am doing a new thing! Now it springs up; do you not perceive it? I am making a way in the wilderness and streams in the wasteland."

Isaiah 43:18–19 (NIV)

This is a true story. When I was in my financial wilderness, I had a dream that I was driving a car and trying to get somewhere. I was not in danger, and it first appeared to me that I was making some progress, but I had a big problem. Despite what I thought, I was not making any progress at all.

Proverbially, I was going nowhere fast because I kept looking in the rearview mirror. How was I going to safely follow the road and the path laid out for me if I constantly kept my eyes focused on the rearview mirror and what was behind me? Anyone who has been behind the steering wheel knows this is a recipe for disastrous failure, an accident waiting to happen. It is impossible to go forward, making safe progress, if you are only focused on the rearview.

When the Scripture tells us to forget the former things and not dwell on the past, it is not like God is telling us that these things did not happen to us; He is saying there is something new He wants to do for us. If our focus is solely on the past, we will miss the restoration of God's highest purpose for our lives. My dream did not warrant any profound interpretation. God had made it plain and simple. He was telling me to stop looking back at the past. God wanted me to fix my eyes on Jesus because He can and will do a new thing. He is the Author and Finisher of our faith (Hebrews 12:2 KJV).

CHAPTER 12 - JOURNEY POINT TO PONDER

On our wilderness journey, we carry heartache and deep disappointment in ourselves and others. We spend valuable time nursing those wounds, trying to mend our broken hearts, and getting stuck in the past. We spend too much time looking in the rearview mirror. God is letting us know that we do not have to look back but, with faith and trust, look forward to a brighter future in Him. He is the God of Restoration.

CHAPTER 12 - GUIDE POST QUESTIONS

1. What are the things in your "rearview mirror" to release to God?
2. List a few areas of your life where God is working behind the scenes for you.
3. What have you learned about God that gives you confidence about your future?

Peaceful
Power In The
Wilderness

13

"I have told you all this so that you may have peace in me. Here on earth you will have many trials and sorrows. But take heart, because I have overcome the world."

– John 16:33 (NLT)

Though it has felt like a million years, and we may not have liked one minute of our wilderness experience, we can take solace in the valuable life lessons we learned from our time in the barren wasteland. As we traveled on wilderness roads filled with deep potholes of loss, overwhelming frustration, and unexpected disappointment, it has been an emotional roller coaster. Today, having come this far by faith, we know our journey with God was not an exercise in futility. Not one step along the way has been in vain. He has done everything with divine intent so that His plans for our highest purpose can be fulfilled by Him alone.

There is no lost cause in God's master plan. Not at all.

Nothing that draws us closer to God and elevates us to His

highest purpose is a waste. We may have absolutely hated the route we had to take—the twists and turns, stops and starts—but the means have justified the end. We can consider ourselves blessed and favored to have been chosen to go through—all the way through. To be given another chance to pick up the pieces of our shattered dreams and be a recipient of the outpouring of God's grace and mercy is a remarkable gift of love. We will never be able to forget what this experience has meant to us.

Like the Israelites, this is what we can say to each other. We will call it our testimony.

> "Remember how the Lord your God led you all the way in the wilderness these forty years, to humble and test you in order to know what was in your heart, whether or not you would keep his commands. He humbled you, causing you to hunger and then feeding you with manna, which neither you nor your ancestors had known, to teach you that man does not live on bread alone but on every word that comes from the mouth of the Lord. Your clothes did not wear out and your feet did not swell during these forty years."
>
> (Deuteronomy 8:2–4 NIV)

During our wilderness experience, we may have lost significant material possessions, professional status, financial security, good health, and dear loved ones. Still, God has used each of these heartbreaking moments to help us see Him more clearly. He has picked up the broken shards, helped us not to get cut by the sharp edges, and given us a new perspective. God mended our broken hearts. He gathered the fragments so nothing would be lost as we willingly pursued His highest purpose. Today, we are under new management, and we are thankful for each lesson learned every step of the wilderness way.

We may have seen our Heavenly Father as an irrational, punitive God who is just waiting for an opportunity to reprimand us and make our lives miserable, but that's the wrong portrait. I had a friend once tell me their picture of God was like a man on a farm chasing a chicken with a hatchet, ready to chop its head off—not a pretty picture. This kind of deceptive mindset can keep us bound by fear. It will make us believe we are unworthy of God's love. Nothing could be further from the truth. God's wilderness training is not a cruel punishment but a loving correction to bring us to His highest purpose. The God we have been talking about corrects us in love to keep us in His protective care. He does this to safeguard us in the same way a good parent holds their child's hand and teaches them to look both ways before crossing the street. As He graciously led us through a dark and barren wilderness, we came to realize that God was bringing us to a better place. All along, He was leading us to a good place:

"For the Lord your God is bringing you into a good land—a land with brooks, streams, and deep springs gushing out into the valleys and hills; a land with wheat and barley, vines and

fig trees, pomegranates, olive oil, and honey; a land where bread will not be scarce and you will lack nothing; a land where the rocks are iron and you can dig copper out of the hills. When you have eaten and are satisfied, praise the Lord your God for the good land he has given you."

(Deuteronomy 8:7–10 NIV)

Some of us knew from the beginning how we landed in the wilderness. God desperately wanted to gain our attention to bring us back from the brink of self-destruction. For others, our secure and peaceful lives were sideswiped by no fault of our own. An unexpected change of events—a family death, job loss, or health crisis—turned our world upside down. The damaging consequences threw us into a chaotic downward spiral. We roamed in the wilderness, bewildered, seeking a way out.

We discovered the only way out was to go all the way through. We could not give up. We realized we were not alone. God was our trustworthy guide. He guided us around our stumbling blocks and made them stepping stones. We learned that our brokenness could be used to help someone else. We recognize we may have been broken to be made a blessing.

So, after a million years, we leave the wilderness behind, shaking off the dust and thanking God with grateful hearts and an overflow of appreciation for what He has done. We have learned that while life may be filled with memorable good times, there have been occasions where we have struggled to see our way. Yet, God has brought us out of the unfruitful places we aimlessly wandered in, where we were lost and confused, with great patience. He has taught us to embrace His highest purpose for our lives. We have experienced transformation. We will never forget it.

> *"Be careful that you do not forget the Lord your God, failing to observe his commands, his laws and his decrees that I am giving you this day. Otherwise, when you eat and are satisfied, when you build fine houses and settle down, and when your herds and flocks grow large and your silver and gold increase and all you have is multiplied, then your heart will become proud and you will forget the Lord your God, who brought you out of Egypt, out of the land of slavery. He led you through the vast and dreadful wilderness, that thirsty and waterless land, with its venomous snakes and scorpions. He brought you water out of hard rock. He gave you manna to eat in the wilderness, something your ancestors had never known, to humble and test you so that in the end it might go well with you. You may say to yourself, 'My power and the strength of my hands have produced this wealth for me.' But remember the Lord your God, for it is he who gives you the ability to produce wealth, and so confirms his covenant, which he swore to your ancestors, as it is today."*

> *(Deuteronomy 8:11–18 NIV)*

When we finally complete whatever project we commit our hearts and minds to fulfilling, there is a sense of jubilee and such joy for what we have accomplished and overcome. You want to do your happy dance because you know there were times you didn't think you would make it, and honestly, like Elijah, you did not even want to try to make it, but your faith in the "God process" has brought you to the here and now!

At this moment, we can briefly look back, without fixating on the rearview mirror, and recognize there was an Architect with plans and purposes uniquely designed for us. Jesus tells us that we will have trials and sorrows on earth, but we can have peace with Him in our lives. He admonishes us to take heart and really believe that He has overcome the world, so in Him, we can trust that all of our concerns, challenges, and issues will be addressed.

Even if it still feels like it's been a million years, we are not alone. We have never been left to our own devices, abandoned to wander in a vast wilderness without the necessary sustenance to sustain us. Jesus has assured us that everything we need can be found in Him, as we are lovingly guided to fulfill His highest purpose for our lives.

As we leave the wilderness, we will never be the same. Even if we come to another wilderness season, we will remember the goodness of our God. He brought us through once; He can do it again.

Closing
Prayer

14

Heavenly Father,

I praise and thank You for being the all-powerful and perfect God with an everlasting love for me. You have been my Guide. You have led me through dangerous and unforeseen circumstances that tried to destroy my heart, mind, body, and soul. I was wandering and lost in a vast wasteland, wondering who I could turn to for help. You have taught me to walk by faith and not by sight. You reminded me that You would never leave or forsake me. Yes, You have been with me every step of the wilderness way, even when I did not recognize and acknowledge Your presence. I am thankful for the wilderness experience and every lesson You taught me.

Now, I understand that it is at times like this that I come to know You better and to love You more. No matter where I am on this journey, I desire to fulfill Your highest purpose for my life.

Lord, where I have fallen short of Your plans and purposes for my life, I repent and ask Your forgiveness. From this day forward, I desire to dedicate my life to You and follow Your plan for me. Help me not to be afraid of the future and to put all my trust in You.

I give You all the glory and praise for what You have already done and what You are going to do.

In Jesus' Name,

Amen

ACKNOWLEDGMENTS

I must begin my acknowledgments with praise and thanksgiving to Jesus Christ for guiding me every step of the way. He is the love of my life. This book is an offering unto Him, and I take no credit other than being a willing vessel open to the leading of the Holy Spirit.

It has been said it takes a whole village to raise a child, and through this writing process, I have learned it takes a lot of caring people to bring a novice book project to the publishing finish line.

I would love to thank everyone personally, but I would need a couple of extra pages to recognize each by name and to appreciate your unique contribution to my life. Please know my spirit is overwhelmed with gratitude for your willingness to share in this labor of love.

This writing journey officially gained traction after an exhaustive search for a Christian editor.

I was blessed to find an experienced and respected editor named Ginger Kolbaba. She gave me an initial glimmer of hope and a vote of confidence when she decided to work with me after reviewing my first draft. Shockingly, she when home to be with the Lord shortly after we began the project. While our connection was brief, I am thankful that she saw my potential and greatly encouraged me as a writer.

I eventually found another Christian editor, Melanie Chitwood, who agreed to take me on as a client after reviewing the manuscript still in its rough form. Melanie's contributions to this book have been invaluable, providing order and focus that had eluded me until I received her insightful direction. As a first-time long-form writer, I could not have asked for a better, more caring editor, and I am deeply grateful for her dedication to this process. Her expertise, kind heart, and grace were evident as she helped me navigate the editorial learning curve. I believe she was heaven-sent.

Special thanks must also be given to a few people who came along to help move the manuscript to its next evolution, preparing it for a public debut. Alice Cameron, James Alexander, and Kathleen Blade took valuable time out of their busy schedules to read the manuscript and give me important feedback. Jermaine Anderson and Jonathan Banks patiently answered questions about self-publishing and gave creative design input. And one person, who shall remain nameless (you know who you are) surprised me, on two separate occasions, with an envelope of cash to keep the editorial process moving forward. Your generosity, patience, and guidance have not gone unnoticed, and I am grateful to each of you.

A special thank you to Mary Goins Richardson, who enthusiastically promised to host a book launch party though I was still desperately trying to pull it all together. Her willingness to plan an event for a work in progress gave me a fresh boost of confidence and a good nudge to finish the book. Sooner than later.

I must acknowledge a few people with heartfelt appreciation because they profoundly influenced my walk with the Lord, and now rest from their labors with Him. Pastors Henry and Effie Soles, Mother Lorraine Johnson, Evangelist Rosemary Blackwell, Mother Consuella York, Mother Fredabelle Martin, Mother Alice Gogins, Apostle Richard D. Henton, and Pastor Julia Coleman. As a great cloud of witnesses, I hope they know their labor was not in vain.

For those still on the "battlefield for my Lord," I recognize and honor Eloise Widgeon, who years ago asked me something that changed my life forever. Her question was simple, why don't you seek the Lord? The rest is spiritual history and the genesis of my decades-long journey with Jesus. We all need someone in our lives to ask the question.

I can't forget Mother Jenny Matthews, Dr. Pernell Hewing of The Sanctuary, Dr. Joyce Wallace of Sceptre Ministries, Felicia Graves of Bethesda Hope Ministries, Carol Owens Ford of Women of Worth Ministries, Helen Mitchell of Wisdom Ministries, Bishop Horace Smith, M.D., and First Lady Susan Davenport Smith of Apostolic Faith Church, Alanna and Bonnie Moulds, Mother Venetta McLean, Pam Morris-Walton, and Deanna Reed Foster, each of them have set beautiful examples of Godly faithfulness. Along the way, Rosemary Spann, Donna Wilson, Brenda Thompson, Laurie Jordan, and Winsome Fenton have all graciously indulged my flights of fancy and subtly kept tabs on me. I must also send a shout-out to the Elevated Book Club founded by Alice Cameron. Our monthly intergenerational get-togethers introduced me to different genres of books I would have overlooked without their suggestions. Our book list, carefully cultivated and democratically voted on, has kept me from getting stuck in a reading rut and generated some lively discussions. All of you on this row call greatly inspire me.

Mother Eddie Mae Carter has been my spiritual mother, the first prayer group member, and faithful intercessor from day one when we met over twenty years ago. Thank you, Mother Carter, for allowing me to be one of your daughters, taking me under your wings, and freely sharing your love and wisdom.

I would be remiss if I did not thank two devoted friends who have been my biggest cheerleaders. Rosemary Culver and I have been friends since the fifth grade. We have lived in separate time zones, seven hundred miles apart for the last four decades. We see each other once a year for a half-day during the Christmas holidays. Yet, she has been a consistent presence in my life. A true sister in the Lord providing wise counsel and a generous dose of laughter. She also has the foresight to know exactly when to call or send a "checking on you" text.

My other cheerleader, Linda Gerber, whom I have known for

over forty years, is the first friend I made when I moved to Chicago to take a job at a local television station. We didn't even work in the same department, but we have bonded over a love for theater, tea time, and supporting each other's community service endeavors. Both women made me feel that I could accomplish anything, even when procrastination and self-doubt wanted to overtake me. I am blessed to know them.

Thanks and appreciation to Marcia Price Penn and Elizabeth Price Obiekwe, my baby sister and oldest niece, respectively. We have a weekly Sunday night appointment for family prayer, and they often ask, "How's the book coming along?" Marcia and Elizabeth never failed to remember me and the project in prayer. I appreciate their loving commitment to lifting up our family and friends every week.

To the rest of my family, all the Rawlins, Big John, Cynthia, John III, Henri and Jessica Smith, and the remainder of the Price tribe scattered around the country, thank you for your love and support. Y'all know all about our wilderness journey. Thank you for always providing a safe place to land and call home.

A special loving appreciation to everyone in the New Thing Ministries Monday Night Prayer & Bible Study group. From the early days in my second-floor office loft, Janet Gogins, Chester Singleteary, Chari Goodloe, Burcy Hines, Paulette Hollingsworth, Kacy Rush, Nadine Johnson, Roxanne Willis, and Janice Beckett have connected with the ministry. We have been coming together for prayer and bible study one way or the other for the last twenty years. To all my new brothers and sisters on the Monday night teleconference prayer call, thank you for your commitment to faithfully seeking the Lord with us and still believing He hears and answers prayers.

Finally, my five-star computer guy patiently dug through an overflowing box of pre-owned laptop computers to find a perfect fit for my first writing project. Aware that I was budget conscious, he was kind enough to give me a good discount and took special care to bring it up to speed. I promised to give him a shout-out in the book, so thank you, N.A., for your consideration and patience in my search for a decent computer that would not crash the budget or the manuscript.

In closing, if there are any omissions, please charge them to my head, not my heart. I am grateful beyond measure, and I love each of you more than I can say! Thank you for your prayers and your presence in my life. I am blessed to be on this journey of life with you

For More Information
www.amillionyearsbook.com

www.ingramcontent.com/pod-product-compliance
Lightning Source LLC
LaVergne TN
LVHW051231080426
835513LV00016B/1527